Records of the
Department of Indian Affairs
at Library and Archives Canada
A Source for Genealogical Research

Bill Russell, Archivist

MULTI PATRIAE
PRIORES ❖ MULTAE

Toronto
The Ontario Genealogical Society
Second Edition, 2004

Further copies of this book and information about the society can be obtained by writing to:

The Ontario Genealogical Society

102 - 40 Orchard View Boulevard

Toronto, ON, Canada M4R 1B9

Library and Archives Canada Cataloguing in Publication

Russell, Bill, 1951-
   Records of the Department of Indian Affairs at Library and Archives
Canada : a source for genealogical research / Bill Russell. — 2nd ed.

Previous ed. published under title: Records of the federal Department of
   Indian Affairs at the National Archives of Canada.
Includes bibliographical references and index.
ISBN 0-7779-2145-6

1. Indians of North America—Canada—Genealogy. 2. Indians of North
America—Canada—Archival resources. 3. Canada. Indian and Northern Affairs Canada—Archives.
4. Library and Archives Canada. I. Ontario Genealogical Society. II. Russell, Bill, 1951- . Records of
the federal Department of Indian Affairs at the National Archives of Canada. III. Title.

E78.C2R87 2005   929'.1'08997071   C2005-900358-8

Thanks to the Archives of Ontario and Paul D. McIlroy, Reference Archivist, for permission to adapt their Pathfinder *Aboriginal Peoples in the Archives: A Guide to Sources in the Archives of Ontario* for use in this volume.

Published by
The Ontario Genealogical Society
40 Orchard View Boulevard, Suite 102
Toronto, Ontario M4R 1B9
Tel. 416-489-0734
Fax 416-489-9803
provoffice@ogs.on.ca
www.ogs.on.ca
Published with assistance from the Ontario Ministry of Culture.

Contents

List of Illustrations

Cover
A composite designed by BG Communications using the portrait of Sa Ga Yeath Qua Pieth Tow, fl. 1710, and the portrait sitting of Privates David Lands, Philip Pelly and William Semia [left to right], taken c.1918 and used as part of the illustration on page 36.

List of Abbreviations

ATIP	Access to Information and Privacy legislation
DBS	Dominion Bureau of Statistics [now Statistics Canada]
DIA	Department of Indian Affairs [precursor of DIAND]
DIAND	Department of Indian Affairs and Northern Development [now replaced by Indian and Northern Affairs Canada, INAC]
DMD	Department of Militia and Defence [forerunner of the DND]
DND	Department of National Defence
DSGIA	Deputy Superintendent General of Indian Affairs (1862)
DVA	Department of Veterans' Affairs
GAD	Government Archives Division [of the LAC]
IAB	Indian Affairs Branch [*See* Department of Indian Affairs, DIA]
ICBC	Indian Commissioner for British Columbia
INAC	Indian and Northern Affairs Canada [most current name of DIA]
LAC	Library and Archives Canada
MG	Manuscript Group [for example MG 21 is the reference code for the Haldimand Papers in the LAC]
NA	National Archives of Canada [formerly the PAC, now the LAC]
PAC	Public Archives of Canada [now the LAC]
PMR	Principal's Monthly Report
pt	Part [of a file within a Record Group]
RG	Record Group [for example: RG 10 is the reference code for the records of the DIA; RG 29 is the reference code for the records of Health and Welfare Canada
SSA	Soldiers' Settlement Act, *See* citation in the bibliography
VLA	Veterans' Land Act, *See* citation in the bibliography
vol(s)	Volume(s) [i.e.: container(s) of records within a Record Group]

Sa Ga Yeath Qua Pieth Tow, fl.1710, said to be related to Joseph Brant and one of the Four Indian Kings painted by John Verelst/Library and Archives Canada/C-092418

Foreword

The genesis of this publication was a presentation made in May 1993 by Bill Russell at the Ontario Genealogical Society Seminar '93, York: The First Hundred. [After some delay, the book appeared in 1998.] … Thanks must be given to Bill Russell for an excellent manuscript, then to a number of readers who made suggestions about its content or its presentation. The first of these is Patricia Kennedy, from Archives Canada, who made excellent suggestions about a number of historical points. Others to be thanked are Norman Baker, Valerie Cole, Audrey Gilchrist and Jeff Stewart, all of whom gave freely of their time in reading the final typeset draft of the manuscript for layout, clarity and readability.

Final thanks must go to Paul D. McIlroy, Reference Archivist at the Archives of Ontario, for allowing us to adapt his Pathfinder, "Aboriginal Sources at the Archives of Ontario," which we used as an appendix. Prepared as a handout for researchers at the Archives of Ontario, these guidelines are helpful for anyone just starting to research Native genealogy.

Clifford Collier, Coordinator
OGS Publishing Division, May 1998

Foreword to the Second Edition

In Spring 2004 the OGS was ready to reprint this useful volume but I felt that because of the reorganization of the National Archives and merging with the National Library, as well as the increased use of computers and the Internet in genealogical research, Bill Russell might want to make some changes. And indeed, he responded "finding aids … have been superseded by our on-line search tool, ArchiviaNet. There are many instances in which reference is made to 'keyword subject indexes' and to search strategies based on such tools — tools no longer used. Indeed, there should probably be some brief general explanation as well of Web-based finding aids. The text was also written just as we were launching into our descriptive shift from the RG/MG to the fonds concept of description."

Then Paul McIlroy sent us an updated version of his contribution, which you will find as Appendix A, "Basic Steps in Researching Your Aboriginal Ancestry." With these updates to the text and the addition of an index, I'm sure you will find our guide a useful tool in your research.

Ruth Chernia, Publisher
Ontario Genealogical Society, January 2005

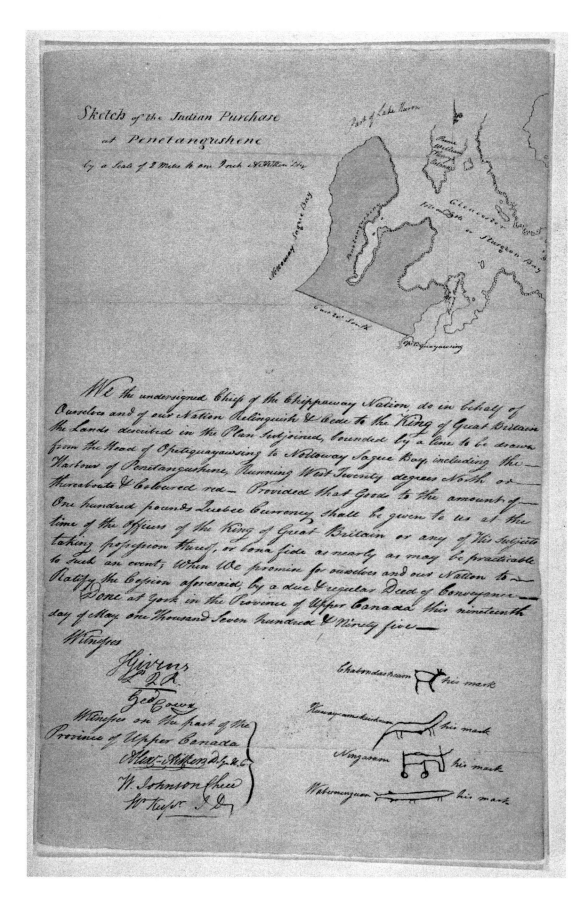

Sketch of the Indian Purchase at Penetanguishene, 19 May 1795/Library and Archives Canada/C-106056

Introduction

The volumes of material in the custody of the Library and Archives Canada that make up the historical collection of the federal Department of Indian Affairs (abbreviated to DIA) are only a part of a wide spectrum of records that help to document the Aboriginal experience since the time of first contact with Europeans and their governments.[*] To some, they are the written testament to all that is bad in the centuries-old Indian/government relationship in Canada. They are the records of "the bureaucracy," presenting a perspective that does not reflect Native cultural values or historical traditions. Moreover, in the politically charged atmosphere surrounding claims negotiations, they are the records of "the other side" in what is, essentially, an adversarial situation.

Yet, at the same time, if the numbers of First Nations researchers using these records today are any indication, they are recognized as an important resource for Aboriginal people and, in particular, status Indians. The nature of the historical relationship between the federal government and Indian First Nations has made them so. Since Confederation, constitutional responsibility for Indian/government relations has been consolidated not only within the jurisdiction of one government but also, to a large extent, within the operational mandate of one department. Although that is less true today, with the transfer of functions to other government agencies and, increasingly, devolution to First Nations governments, for much of the past 125 years the DIA has been the government overseer of virtually all aspects of Indian life in Canada.

The Multitude of Records — A Multiplicity of Functions

As a consequence, the DIA records reflect a multiplicity of functions from education to economic development, from the allotment of individual land holdings on reserves to the final adjudication of Indian status. The Department developed as a self-contained agency with officers responsible for a wide range of services for its clientele — the Native peoples. The records created in the process reflect the all-encompassing mandate of its operations. In its role as records creator and keeper, the DIA controlled — in certain spheres — the sole written record for every facet of Indian life, be it legal, social, economic or cultural.

Today, large numbers of First Nations researchers are mining the richness of the DIA seam. The emergence of Aboriginal claims in the last three decades has generated a considerable demand for his-

---

[*] The opinions expressed in this publication are those of the author alone and do not represent the views of Library and Archives Canada.

torical documents. Genealogical research has been an important aspect of claims work for many years. The determination of who was, and who was not, an Indian, as defined in the Indian Act, has been a critical factor in many historical claims. More recently, the passage of federal legislation designed to remove discriminatory clauses from the Indian Act has had the effect of creating a veritable genealogical boom as people search for their Aboriginal ancestors in order to document claims to Indian status. The Indian Act as we know it today has gone through many revisions and re-enactments over the years. The second edition of *The Historical Development of the Indian Act* by John Leslie and Ron Maguire and the entry under Indian Act in the Bibliography will give you more details about these changes.[1]

Yet, the historical records of the DIA at Library and Archives Canada also have much to offer the genealogist whose search is not claims-driven but who simply seeks to know more about his or her family's past. These records have considerable potential as a source of information about individuals. I cannot hope to cover in this one volume all the areas that are in the DIA records in which individual-level information will be found. I will, however, attempt to highlight those I consider to be the most important and to offer some guidance, not only as to what the records are, but also how they can be accessed at Library and Archives Canada.

RG 10 Is Not the Only Source

Before proceeding, I must underline that the records described here — Record Group 10 (RG 10) — form the principal and most important, but not the only, resource for Native research. There is a wealth of textual documentary material relating to Aboriginal people available to the genealogist at the Library and Archives Canada. By focusing the area of discussion on those records of a single agency and a single record group, I must leave aside both those documents found in other federal government departments with which Native people came into contact, and the extensive and significant manuscript holdings in the Library and Archives Canada. I give two obvious examples of the latter group that document the roles played by Aboriginal peoples in the economic and social development of this country — the fur trade records and those of the various religious denominations. The richness and extent of these records warrants separate treatment by their own specialists.

The researcher new to the records relating to Aboriginal people could find no better place to begin than with two guides prepared by Bennett McCardle. Her two-volume *Indian History and Claims: A Research Handbook* (Ottawa: Department of Indian Affairs and Northern Development, 1982) is an indispensable tool. A chapter is devoted to "Indian Status, Membership, and Family History." The second work, "Archival Records Relating to Native People in the Public Archives of Canada, the National Library of Canada, and the National Museum of Man: A Thematic Guide" has not yet been published although a copy is available for consultation at the Claims and Historical Research Centre, Department of Indian and Northern Affairs Canada in Ottawa.

I propose to discuss RG 10 in terms of four groups upon whom its documents shed varying intensities of light. The most important of these is, of course, status Indians, those people for whom the Indian Affairs administration exists. I will then mention, very briefly, what RG 10 has to offer or, more to the point, what it does not have to offer to those researching Aboriginal peoples whose status does not come within the meaning of the Indian Act — the Inuit, the Métis and the non-status Indians.

A third group of people whose lives are documented in the holdings of RG 10 are the employees of the administration, both the regular DIA staff at headquarters and in the field, and those whose services were purchased or subsidized by the Department. Finally, the researcher whose ancestor falls within a fourth group, those from the non-Indian population who had dealings with Indians or with the DIA, will also find these records of interest. Examples of these people that spring most easily to mind are those individuals who purchased surrendered Indian lands from the government.

In terms of research potential, what most obviously distinguishes the last three groups from the first is that, for them, RG 10 is not what I would term a principal genealogical source. Rather, what RG 10 offers to those researching these groups is records that will complement and supplement their findings elsewhere. For example, the DIA files documenting the appointment of your grandfather as an Indian agent, or the meticulous monthly reports that he sent to his superiors in Ottawa, will be mostly of interest not for any "tombstone" or vital information they may provide (information you will doubtless already have from other sources) but, rather, for what they say about his life and experiences. For genealogical research involving status Indians, on the other hand, the alternative sources are too often more limited. In such cases, the DIA records found in RG 10 may be the only textual documentation in the lives of individuals — or entire families — for years.

Before turning to a discussion of the content of the records themselves, a few words are required about their creator — the DIA — the manner of their creation and their archival home — RG 10.

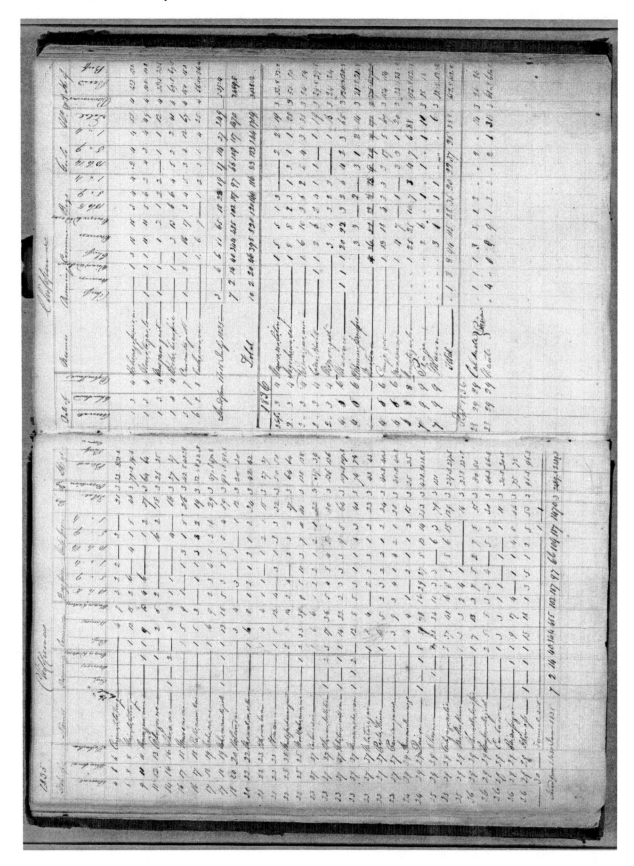

Record of distribution of presents to Chippawas [sic], 1835–1836, showing numbers of chiefs, warriors, women and children and the quantities of presents provided/Library and Archives Canada/C-142541

Chapter One

The Department of Indian Affairs

As an archivist dealing with the records of a relatively complex bureaucracy, I often have to tell researchers that, in order to exploit the holdings most effectively, they must first understand the agency's administrative history, its organizational structure and records-keeping practices, as well as the developments in each over time. Although it is not historically correct to do so, for convenience sake, I will refer throughout this book to the Department of Indian Affairs (abbreviated as DIA). The agency, primarily responsible for Indians and lands reserved for Indians, has found a home in different government departments, indeed with different governments. Until 1860, Indians were the responsibility of the Imperial Government and the management of relations with Native peoples was administered in each colony through the Governor. In that year, this responsibility was transferred to the individual colonies of British North America. In the Province of Canada, administering Indians and their lands was included among the duties of the Crown Lands Department. Once a permanent head, a Deputy Superintendent-General of Indian Affairs (DSGIA), was appointed in 1862, Indian Affairs took on the status equivalent to a branch in that department. Indians became the exclusive responsibility of the federal government at Confederation, but the organizational structure that had been created in the Crown Lands Department of the Province of Canada passed largely intact to federal control, firstly under the ministerial authority of the Secretary of State for Canada, then briefly under the Secretary of State for the Provinces, before being transferred in 1873 to the newly created Department of the Interior. Departmental status was achieved in 1880 and the DIA continued to operate as a department until 1936, although it did not have a separate Minister but reported to Parliament through other Ministers. In 1936, Indian Affairs reverted to branch status within the newly formed Department of Mines and Resources. The Indian Affairs Branch, as it became known, was later transferred to Citizenship and Immigration and then to the Department of Northern Affairs and National Resources before finding its present home within the Department of Indian Affairs and Northern Development (DIAND). Currently, DIAND calls itself Indian and Northern Affairs Canada (INAC). For a more detailed administrative chronology see *Guide to Canadian Ministries Since Confederation* (Ottawa: Public Archives of Canada, 1974).

Eyes glaze over and hearts sink at the thought of wading through "all that bumf" when all they really want is to find what records exist for their grandmother who, family tradition maintains, was an Indian. That this information should exist in a relatively concise form, and be located through straight-forward manipulation of some indexes, is not an entirely unreasonable expectation when you consider the extraordinary control that the DIA exercised historically over the lives of Indian people. The simple truth is that the DIA came to create and maintain records on virtually every aspect of a status Indian's life, from birth to death. Yet, the researcher must never lose sight of the fact that RG 10 includes only the historical record of aspects of Indian life as documented for the purposes of the government. At best, RG 10 provides documentation of those events that were relevant to the DIA and its mandate, and presents the evidence from the perspective of the creator of the records.

Indians, and lands reserved for Indians, were the DIA's business. Yet there is a seeming paradox. To the uninitiated, individuals can seem to be invisible in so many of the records because, with certain important exceptions, the records-keeping systems in place in the DIA were not geared to the identification of the individual and many records are not organized in a manner that makes individual-level research simple. These are records of a bureaucracy that document its functions of administration. Admittedly, it was a bureaucracy that dealt extensively with people, but was an administration nonetheless.

Administrative Convenience

In the filing systems that evolved within the DIA, records have been arranged for administrative convenience, which means primarily by subject. There is the potential for a record of an individual being found in any file, listed under subjects with which that person had dealings with the bureaucracy. If your grandfather attended a residential school, there may be a record of his entering or leaving in an admissions and discharges file and, possibly, even a reference in a school inspector's report. If he was a treaty Indian, chances are good that his name will appear on a treaty annuity paylist. If he was a community leader, there is the possibility of a record of his selection as a chief or band councillor. If he served in the army in World War II and he bought a truck with his Veterans' Land Act[2] grant (abbreviated as VLA), there could be a file documenting that transaction. But you, as the researcher, have to know how the creators of the records kept such information, how they arranged their records and how their filing systems worked, in order to realize the full potential of the material.

Moreover, for much of the first century of federal responsibility for Indians, the basic organizational unit of administration in the DIA was the Agency and, within that, the Band. This structure is reflected in the way the records are arranged. A record of an individual on a given subject may be found in an individual "case file." However, more likely than not — and especially for the period prior to World War II — such a record will reside in a general agency-wide (or band) file and combined with same-subject records of many other people. That file will likely be identified in finding aids only by the agency or band name. Therefore, not only do you need to appreciate the idiosyncrasies of records subject classification, but you must also know what band you are dealing with and what DIA administrative unit was responsible for the affairs of that band, before you can hope to find an appropriate record.

A Centralized Decision-making Agency

The fact that the DIA is a geographically decentralized agency — which is reflected in its records system — adds another layer of complexity to your search. An event relating to an individual, or aspects of that event, may have been documented in either field office or headquarters records, or in both. Historically, the latter scenario is more probable. The DIA, although operationally a geographically decentralized agency, was, until quite recently, very centralized in its decision-making.

At certain periods in its history, the DIA bureaucracy has had three tiers: the headquarters, the agency and an intermediate level known differently in various parts of the country and at different times that broadly corresponds to a regional office. It may be necessary to canvas the records (if they still survive) of all three levels of the bureaucracy in order to obtain as complete a picture of an event as possible. In many cases there will be much duplication among the records at each level. Yet, each office might have added something — material, comments, etc. — to the issue, based upon an action taken at its level only. There is a dangerous tendency, particularly among those new to RG 10, to assume that they have seen everything extant on an issue because they have reviewed the headquarters files. At no time was this true. As a word of caution, with the full-scale decentralization of powers to the regions currently underway in Indian and Northern Affairs Canada (INAC), it will be even less true in the future.

The Relationship Is Changing over Time

The final consideration that requires a general comment is "change-over-time." The relationship between the Indian people and the DIA is not static. Both the services that the DIA has provided to its client, and the manner in which these services have been delivered, have evolved. That evolution mirrored the changing needs and expectations of the principal players and of society-at-large. The records created reflect that evolution. For example, there are few records from the DIA documenting early nineteenth-century Native health issues. The Department did not take a great responsibility for Aboriginal medical care (just as the government did not have the responsibility for the health of the broader population at that time).

In an example of another sort, I have encountered researcher surprise in that RG 10 offers very little in the way of records for the early years of western and, particularly, northern treaties. The simple explanation is that there were few, if any, officers in the area permanently. For example, for many years after the signing of Treaties 8 and 11 — covering parts of northern Alberta, Saskatchewan and British Columbia, and the southern Northwest Territories — the DIA presence was nothing more than the annual treaty-annuity payment visit with the main record being the paying officer's report. Even with the appointment of permanent agents to an area, contacts with remote or nomadic peoples were infrequent and short until well into the twentieth century.

The office of Superintendent of Indian Affairs (created in 1755) was vastly different in terms of both structure and mandate from the agencies inherited by the federal government at Confederation, or the one that exists today. It is not my intention to attempt to trace the evolution of the government's relationship with Aboriginal people but, rather, to selectively highlight certain points at which the relationship underwent important changes in order to suggest the effect that such shifts can have on the nature and extent of records created.

The Native As a Military Ally

The earliest records found in RG 10 today pre-date the creation of the Imperial Indian Department. These are records that the administration that was created in 1755 inherited from earlier contacts between Aboriginal people and European governing authorities in the North American colonies. That aside, taking 1755 as the genesis of the agency that came to be known as the DIA, how can we characterize the Department's mandate and the type of records it created in the course of its work? This period was one of intense colonial rivalry in which both the British and the French vied for support of militarily valuable Indian allies. In this struggle, the British authorities had a particularly difficult juggling task to perform. They had to attempt to mitigate, if not to reconcile, the negative effects of the seemingly mutually exclusive interests of their Indian allies and the territorial expansion of their

American colonists into Indian land. The records that survive in RG 10 from this period have much to do with military policy and strategy, with councils and negotiations between prominent figures in the Indian Department, such as Sir William Johnson, and the Native leaders.

The overriding importance of the Indian as military ally continued to mark its stamp on the relationship through the years of the American rebellion and the struggle for control of the Old Northwest that continued after the peace of 1783. This period is treated with much insight by Robert Allen in *His Majesty's Indian Allies: British Indian Policy in the Defence of Canada, 1774-1815*. The movement of settlement into what would become Upper Canada introduced land as a factor into the relationship. The British authorities had not only to obtain land by means of surrenders from the indigenous population but also to make portions of it available for the use and occupancy of their Six Nations allies who had been displaced from their now American-occupied territory. Much of the record in RG 10 for the period up to the War of 1812 is characterized by dealings for and about the control and use of Indian land, including such documents as petitions, leases and correspondence covering Six Nations Grand River claims or the various treaty and surrender documents by which the land was obtained.

As long as maintaining Indians as military allies was a pillar of Indian Department policy, the annual distribution of presents was the glue that cemented the friendship. It is during this period that lists of distributions of presents to Indian allies appear, documenting a practice begun before the American rebellion and continuing until 1858, long after the military significance of the recipients had dwindled. These lists, of course, are not full nominal lists. The concern of those creating them was with chiefs and warriors, not the names of family members. Yet, it is such lists, illustrated on page 4, that, in later years, provide some of the earliest returns of Native population. RG 10, vol. 708, described as a "census" record, is, in fact, a record of presents distributed to various Native groups in southern Ontario during the period 1830–1836. Most lists record the date of arrival and departure (for visiting Indians), the name of head of family and numbers of other household members, identity of chiefs and warriors, age ranges and rations distributed. Similar records of those entitled to presents in Lower Canada exist for the years 1840–1852 in RG 10, vol. 747, and for Indians in Upper Canada, c.1846–1852 in RG 10, vol. 999A.

After 1814

With the end of war in 1814, the immediate military importance of the Native population largely disappeared. The period up to 1830 could be characterized as one of increasing neglect. Land relations continued to be reflected in the records with petitions and correspondence from white settlers and Natives alike. Issues of social policy, however, were left largely to the church and missionaries. The first schools for Indians, for example, had been established in Upper Canada by Church of England missionaries, shortly after the arrival of the displaced Six Nations. The Moravian Brethren opened a school among the Delaware in 1793. The Methodists were not long in following suit. These institutions were left to the churches and there was little or no interference from the Indian Department. The result, of course, is that the Indian Department did not document school activities.[3] The point to be stressed here is that, for the first seventy-five years of the Indian Department, the nature of the relationship between the agency and the Indians limited the creation of records documenting the activities of individual Indians.

In the face of the growing humanitarian movement in England, a major new policy direction was taken in Indian administration in 1830. Henceforth, in the Canadas at least, (for the policy shift seems to have been largely ignored in Nova Scotia and New Brunswick),[4] the Indian, no longer a valued military ally, was to be protected and "civilized" through the promotion of education, Christianity and agricultural training on reserves. The goal of this policy was assimilation. This policy placed responsibility for a much wider range of aspects of Indian welfare in the hands of the Indian Department. Moving the relationship with the Aboriginal population from one of benign neglect to wardship meant the creation of an increasingly elaborate administrative machinery. With Indian agents placed on reserves, Indian life was more closely monitored than ever before; the result was a great deal more recording of information about the Indian population.

Responsibility for Indians Transferred to the Colonies

The machinery of control was not developed overnight but, by 1860 (the year of transfer of responsibility for Indians to the individual colonies), the policy was firmly entrenched, buttressed by the first pieces of Indian legislation. Acts relating to Indian lands had been passed in both Lower and Upper Canada. Indeed, the first definition in legislation of an "Indian" appeared in An Act for the better protection of the lands and property of the Indians in Lower Canada,[5] passed in 1850. The definition was refined further in legislation passed the following year that also introduced the differentiation between "status" and "non-status" Indians.[6] It was only with the increasingly precise definition of who was (and who was not) an Indian that the need arose to keep good records to differentiate "status" Indians from "non-status" Indians. The goal of eventual assimilation was underlined in 1857 with the passage of An Act to encourage the gradual civilization of the Indian Tribes in this Province, and to amend the Laws respecting Indians,[7] which introduced into statute the concept of "enfranchisement." The first federal legislation was enacted in 1868 and further refined the following year.[8] By 1876, the year in which the first major attempt was made to consolidate legislation relating to Indians into one Act, the relationship had grown sufficiently complex to require an Act of 100 clauses.

Expansion into the West created a whole new dimension to the relationship. The negotiation of seven treaties in six years brought into the DIA fold an Indian population that not only stretched from the head of Lake Superior to the Rocky Mountains but also was still largely nomadic, with a livelihood based upon the hunt. Within a decade, a system of field offices was established, the surveying of reserves had begun and the first endeavours to turn the Native population into farmers was underway. Schools were introduced into the West; indeed, they had been specifically negotiated into the treaties. In subtle and not so subtle ways, the state, through the vehicle of the DIA, came to play an ever-increasing role in Native life.

This process was accelerated during the first half of the twentieth century as the state came to play a more significant role in the lives of the entire Canadian population. Nowhere is this more evident than in social policy. Services provided by charitable organizations or religious institutions came increasingly within the mandate of the state, at one or another of its levels, to perform and document. The "state" for the status Indians was the clientele department — the DIA. Even where other government agencies were created to administer programs for the wider population, it was the DIA (the state agency) that either brought them directly to the Indian (the client) or acted as a filter between the two. The growth in records of the clientele department was phenomenal.

Recent Changes to the DIA

It is only recently (since World War II) that the all-encompassing power of the clientele department has been eroded. While DIA may still fund major services, their delivery has increasingly been transferred to other agencies of government (both federal and provincial) and to First Nations governments themselves. The DIA has moved a long way down the road, away from the status of a clientele department towards that of an inter-governmental affairs agency. It no longer aspires to the ultimate assimilation of Indian people but, rather, to deal with them on a government-to-government basis. This changing relationship is reflected in the records being created today in the DIA and, more importantly, in the fact that programs are devolving, along with their records, from the control of the department to that of First Nations governments.

Extract from a census of the Band of Micmacs, Shelburne County, Nova Scotia, 1900. A full nominal census including age range, religion, and family relationship/Library and Archives Canada/C-142524

Chapter Two

RG 10 — The Indian and Inuit Affairs Program *Sous-fonds*

Having said something in the previous chapter about the nature of the records creator, and of the records created, it remains to discuss briefly their archival home — the Indian and Inuit Affairs Program *sous-fonds* and the Government Archives Division (GAD) at LAC, which has responsibility for the records. At the time of publication of the first edition of this guide, Library and Archives Canada had just recently launched changes in the system used to describe its holdings. These changes are now firmly in place. The Record Group (RG) system of archival description has been replaced by one based on the concept of the archival *fonds*. For descriptive purposes, one no longer speaks of "Record Group 10 — Records Relating to Indian Affairs." The records that were formerly described as belonging to RG 10 now constitute the records of the Indian and Inuit Affairs Program *sous-fonds* of the Department of Indian Affairs and Northern Development *fonds*. That said, Library and Archives Canada has retained "RG 10" as a reference code for these records. LAC clients continue to use the "RG 10" designation to identify records for physical retrieval. Physical container numbers have not changed. Hence, a record previously known as, for example, RG 10, volume 708, must still be identified as such by clients wishing to consult the record or obtain copies. For this reason, all references to specific records in this edition of the guide continue to cite those records according to their "RG 10" designation.

The Government Archives Division is responsible for the custody of the textual, micrographic and electronic records of the federal government that have been determined to have archival or historical value.[9] Within the Government Archives Division, records are described within archival *fonds* and, within these *fonds*, in *sous-fonds*, series and sub-series. A *fonds* is defined as "the whole of the documents, regardless of form or medium, automatically and organically created and/or accumulated and used by a particular individual, family, or corporate body in the course of that creator's activities or functions."[10] In some cases this means that the records of an entire federal department will be found in one *fonds*; in others, a *fonds* may consist of the records of a smaller unit of a department, such as a branch. At LAC, the Indian and Inuit Affairs Program is classified as a *sous-fonds*, the parent Department of Indian Affairs and Northern Development having the status of a *fonds*.

The Indian and Inuit Affairs Program *sous-fonds* (RG 10) draws together records that display an administrative continuity going back to the mid-eighteenth century. Since the creation of the Canadian state in 1867, responsibility for Indians and lands reserved for the Indians has been attached to an assortment of ministries. Yet, through all this time, the records have travelled, by and large, with the responsibility. From the first transfer in 1907 to what was then the Archives Branch of the Department of Agriculture, DIA holdings at LAC have grown to over 14,000 volumes of textual records and over forty electronic data files. Even though that makes RG 10 one of the larger holdings of federal government records in LAC custody, there are significant gaps in the collection. (I am using the term "gap" here to refer to records not in the LAC holdings but which would be considered to be of historical value. This is distinct from that class of record that has no permanent value and is routinely destroyed as part of good records management procedure.) The most obvious is not a gap in Library and Archives Canada holdings at all, but is often perceived as one. I refer to those records still in DIAND custody.

Some Records Still in the Custody of DIAND

While the Library and Archives Canada is ultimately responsible for the disposition of records of the federal government, there is no hard and fast government-wide rule about when the transfer of records from the various departments to the LAC takes place. Records are created for operational reasons and, as long as they continue to be required by a department to enable it to perform its mandate, they will normally be retained by the department. Those records of historical value will be identified for eventual transfer to the Library and Archives Canada and the circumstances and timing of that transfer negotiated between the two agencies. It is not generally the practice of the Library and Archives Canada to acquire records that are still of active use in a department. In the case of Indian Affairs records, there remains a significant amount of material, some dating back to the nineteenth century, that has yet to be transferred to LAC custody. If the records you wish to consult fall within this category, contact the DIAND Access to Information and Privacy Coordinator or the Claims and Historical Research Centre.

It is true that gaps do exist from the simple fact that some records have not survived. Although public records have been part of the mandate of the Library and Archives Canada since early in the twentieth century, it is only since World War II that the institution has come to play a significant role in government-wide records management, and the acquisition and preservation of federal government records of historical value. Before that time, individual departments acted largely on their own regarding their records. The researcher today is remarkably fortunate in that the DIA took as good care of its historical record as it did and that so much of it could ultimately find its way into LAC. For many years the DIA refused to authorize the destruction of any record at all and only reluctantly succumbed when the pressures of the paper burden became too great. I have written about pre–World War I DIA records retention and disposal policies. There is also information about the post war period.[11]

Some Records Did Not Survive

However, the care that was taken with regard to the retention of headquarters records does not seem to have been duplicated in the field, despite the fact that there were official policies that required strict control of records destruction there. As a result, it is in its holdings from field offices, especially for the period between the two world wars, that RG 10 is particularly weak. There is virtually nothing of the local record of Indian Affairs in Atlantic Canada prior to 1940, for example. Agents, often engaged in DIA service on a part-time basis only, came and went and records of their activities were lost in the process.

The hard fact is simply that there are records the fate of which will never be known. To the researcher, of course, that is one of the most difficult things to accept. There is a natural tendency to assume that if you look long enough for something you will find it. Logic and knowledge of the bureaucracy may indicate that such and such a record had to have been created in the DIA. Indeed, there may be absolute proof that it did at one time exist; contemporary indexes or surviving records may refer to the document you require. Yet it may be lost forever. There are finding aids in both DIAND's record office and in RG 10 that positively identify certain records that have been destroyed. While it may be cold comfort to know that the record you are searching for has not survived, that information will at least save you wasted effort. However, there are many other records the fate of which cannot be documented.

Rather than dwell on what might have been, however, it is better to concentrate on what has survived and can be used today at the Library and Archives Canada. At this point, some general words about how to use RG 10, its finding aids and microfilm, and about government access policy and procedures are in order.

Utilizing the Finding Aids

Once you have determined that the Indian and Inuit Affairs Program *sous-fonds* may be useful to your research, the best introduction into the records is the *sous-fonds* descriptive record found in the General Inventory database available on the LAC Web site **www.collectionscanada.ca** using the on-line research tool ArchiviaNet. This descriptive record provides a brief administrative history of the record-creator — the Indian and Inuit Affairs Program and its historical antecedents — as well as information about the scope and content of the *sous-fonds*. It provides hypertext links to the various records series that go to make up the *sous-fonds* as well as a link to a description of the parent *fonds* — the Department of Indian Affairs and Northern Development.

The various series descriptions provide further information about the scope and content of each particular series, including an indication of the range of volumes (containers) in which the records are stored, whether or not the records have been microfilmed, whether the records are stored at LAC headquarters in Ottawa or in one of the regional Federal Records Centres across Canada and which of the over 500 finding aids one should consult for a more detailed description of the material. Although many of the finding aids exist in paper format only, some of the most frequently used have been automated and can be searched on-line, again using ArchiviaNet. Some finding aids have also been microfilmed, although microfilm versions have largely fallen into disuse as their format does not readily accommodate updating. Where finding aids exist in paper format only, photocopies can usually be obtained at standard LAC charges.

A large portion of the RG 10 record, itself, has also been microfilmed and much of that film can be borrowed through the inter-institutional loan network. In the early 1970s, in response to the pressing demand from Aboriginal people for records to be made available for claims research, large quantities of material were transferred from DIAND to the LAC. In order to further facilitate access to these records, a team of DIAND officers reviewed them file by file, opening to research as much as government access policy of the day permitted. For its part, the LAC then undertook an indexing and microfilming project of a magnitude unprecedented in the institution's history. The result is that a significant percentage of the collection is available to be consulted off-site. As well, many libraries across the country have now purchased portions of this microfilmed record, thus increasing its availability further. To date, virtually no RG 10 records are available on-line, although projects for digitizing records can be expected in the near future.

Access to Information and Privacy legislation (ATIP)

Anyone who is searching in RG 10 for individual-level information, particularly of a more recent vintage, will eventually encounter the federal Access to Information and Privacy legislation (hereafter abbreviated as ATIP).[12] There is a certain amount of misunderstanding about this legislation and its effect upon records in the custody of the Library and Archives Canada. The first point to remember is that the federal government had a policy that restricted access to records long before the proclamation of ATIP laws. Generally, material at the LAC, access to which was unrestricted when the legislation came into effect (1 July 1983), has remained fully open to research. Records that were restricted under pre-ATIP policies must now be reviewed prior to their release, under the terms of the ATIP acts. Records that have been acquired by the LAC since proclamation of the legislation — and that had not been reviewed and opened under the terms of the acts by the transferring department — must be reviewed, prior to release, by the LAC access officers.

There are portions of RG 10, significant for genealogical research, that can be consulted only in a manner consistent with the terms of the ATIP laws, and only at LAC headquarters. In the majority of cases it is the Privacy Act that comes into play. This legislation "protects the privacy of individuals with respect to personal information about themselves held by a government institution and provides individuals with a right of access to such information."[13]

It comes as no surprise that the DIA has, historically, created a great quantity of records that contain personal information, the unwarranted disclosure of which could represent an invasion of privacy. The determination of Indian status and the events affecting that status have been fundamental to DIA operations. Only those who meet the status qualifications of the Indian Act are entitled to benefit from that legislation. Over the past century and a quarter, the DIA has developed elaborate mechanisms to document who does, and who does not, qualify for Indian status. There is much in such records that reflects upon births, marriages, adoptions, enfranchisements, family structures and the movement of people, some of which is information of a highly personal nature. In addition, a clientele agency such as the DIA, by the very nature of the wide range of social programs it has operated, has created a great quantity of records relating to the socio-economic conditions of individual Indians. A whole range of records containing personal information which, for other citizens might be found scattered through a number of government agencies, are concentrated in the files of the DIA. School and medical records, employment and personal financial data or documentation concerning wills and estates come readily to mind as examples.

The special circumstances that require those involved in Aboriginal claims research to consult records that contain personal information were taken into consideration in the drafting of the Privacy Act. Section 8(2)(k) of the Act provides that personal information under the control of a government institution may be disclosed to "any association of aboriginal people, Indian band, government institution, or part thereof, or to any person acting on behalf of such association, band, institution or part thereof, for the purpose of researching or validating the claims, disputes or grievances of any of the aboriginal peoples of Canada."

Before Access Is Granted

In order to benefit from the terms of this clause of the Act, the researcher must meet two conditions. He or she must produce "written accreditation from the responsible officers of the association, band or institution stating that the researcher is acting on behalf of that organization with respect to a specific claim, dispute or grievance" (what this normally involves is the production of a Band Council Resolution) and agree "in writing not to use the information for any purpose other than that for which access is granted."[14] For those who meet the terms of Section 8(2)(k) of the Privacy Act, I offer this advice to ensure that your research runs smoothly: to avoid the disappointment, to say nothing of the expense of a wasted trip, do not appear at the LAC without your proper accreditation. If you have any doubt, contact the Access to Information and Privacy Division before setting out.

To those whose genealogical work is not related to the research or validation of an Aboriginal claim, dispute or grievance, this clause of the Act, of course, provides no benefit. Should you find, in consulting LAC finding aids, that the record you wish to view is "restricted," you are wise to apply informally — in the first instance — to have the record reviewed. It is possible that its closure stems simply from the fact that it was transferred to the LAC after proclamation of the Act, and has not yet been reviewed. Or, it was restricted under pre-ATIP policy and its access status has never been reviewed under the terms of the new legislation. It is also possible that part of the record can be made available to you even if certain portions have to remain closed. The simple message from these comments is that you should not be intimidated by ATIP legislation; exercise your rights under ATIP law.

It is hoped that the preceding remarks have set the stage for what is to follow: a discussion of the records themselves and how they can be used in your search for those individuals included within the four groups identified earlier — status Indians, non-status Indians and other Aboriginal peoples, employees of the administration and the non-Indian population who had dealings with the native peoples or with the DIA itself.

Making the Treaty. A group of Indians gathered to hear the Treaty Commissioners at the signing of Treaty 9 in northern Ontario. Flying Post [Ontario, 1906]/Library and Archives Canada/PA-59600

Chapter Three

RG 10 Sources for Individual Status Indians

The overwhelming importance of the resolution of claims and status issues does much to shape the nature of genealogical research in RG 10. There may well be (and I hope there is) an army of researchers who are tracing their Aboriginal ancestry for what I can only call the sheer pleasure of learning about their heritage, both personal and collective. Examples might be those people writing community histories or biographies of prominent members of their bands. In all but a very few isolated cases, however, that is not the *immediate* goal of the researchers that I, as an RG 10 archivist have encountered. Rather, the genealogical researcher I have seen is usually pursuing one of two ends: those who need individual-level information in order to establish their own or a relative's Indian status to the satisfaction of the federal government, so that they can be officially recognized as status Indians; or those whose genealogical research is focused on band (and usually land) claims and the need to determine precise historical population figures.

I stress immediate here because it is doubtless the case that for a great number of those seeking to establish Indian status through genealogical research, that in itself is not the ultimate goal but the means. It is the cultural identification that comes from "official" recognition of status that is surely important to many who pursue this research. *Impacts of the 1985 Amendments to the Indian Act (Bill C-31) Summary Report*[15] shows the results of a survey done in 1990 of 2000 registrants for status under Bill C-31. Forty percent said their reason for registering was related to personal identity; 21% gave "culture or a sense of belonging" as their reason; 17% cited "correction of injustice"; 7% cited "aboriginal rights." The education benefits/grants obtained through status were mentioned by 14% of those surveyed, and non-insured health benefits by 12%.

I hasten to add that, for others in the Aboriginal community, this "official" recognition carries much less meaning in that it is just that, recognition under a law that is not of their making and that reflects customs that are not relevant to their cultural traditions. There are Aboriginal people who are eligible to register their status under the Indian Act but refuse to, secure in the knowledge that they do not need the federal government to tell them whether or not they are Indian.

Official Recognition As Status Indians

The emergence of the first group in large numbers is a recent phenomenon and can be attributed to the passage of legislation amending the Indian Act in 1985. In doing so, the federal government created a genealogical research boom the size of which even it did not anticipate. In that year, the Indian Act was amended to remove sections that were recognized to be incompatible with the Canadian Charter of Rights and Freedoms. The amendments, among other things, removed from the Act discrimination on the basis of gender and did away with the enfranchisement provisions. Subsequent regulations provided the mechanisms by which people who had lost or were denied Indian status (especially Indian women who had lost status through marriage to non-Indians) could apply for registration.[16] What this means, of course, is that research is needed to be able to document Indian status. The bulk of this research is carried out within DIAND in a unit established specifically to deal with registration applications. The people an archivist at the LAC is more likely to encounter are those who either want to verify the facts of their case independently of the government or those whose application cannot be processed because of incomplete documentation.

Tracing Band and Land Claims Information

The second type of researcher needing individual-level information and who is frequently encountered at LAC is the land claims researcher. An example of the type of claim that requires genealogical tracing is treaty land entitlement, an issue in those parts of the West covered by treaties. The western treaties stipulated that a land base would be reserved for the exclusive use of Indian people and further stated that the size of reserves would be determined by population. Under these circumstances, a precise count of the number of eligible status Indians has a direct relationship to the land-base size. In some instances, reserve land was never set aside. Even in those cases where it was, there remains much ground for dispute. Reserves were not always allocated in a size commensurate with the population. Many western bands, to say nothing of DIAND and provincial governments, have carried out extensive genealogical research in order to document claims for an increased reserve land base. The provincial governments' stake in the settlement of such claims is very real since Crown lands were transferred from the federal government to the Prairie provinces in 1930 with the proviso that lands would be made available to the federal government thereafter to meet the as-yet-unresolved needs for Indian land. It is the provinces, then, that share the interest in what lands will be made available for the settlement of treaty entitlement claims. This is not a straightforward task when you consider the unsettled nature of the western Indian population in the first decades after treaty, the upheavals of 1885, and the movement of individuals in and out of treaty status and between bands.

Resources Dealing with All Canadians

The first point to bear in mind when beginning a trace of an individual status Indian is that the available pool of written records can be divided broadly into two. First are those dealing with the broader Canadian population — records that captured information about Indian and non-Indian alike. Second are those unique to status Indians or, more precisely, those the creation of which is unique to the DIA.

Given the importance placed today upon documenting Indian status and establishing reliable figures of the populations eligible to benefit in land settlements, certain types of records are obviously more heavily used than others. Six of these record types will be covered first: the Indian Register, census records, "Indian censuses," vital statistics records, paylists and membership and status-related records. RG 10 does include other types of records that, although not heavily used in claims/status research, do document the activities of individual Indians and may well be useful for genealogical needs. These will be referred to later under the somewhat artificial categories of individual records of economic activity, social records, education records, individual reserve land and property records and administration and military records.

The Indian Register

It often amazes researchers, given the central concern which the DIA had for identifying who was, and who was not, a status Indian, that it is only just over fifty years ago that the department established its first centralized master list of status Indians. The Indian Act of 1951 decreed that an Indian Register must be maintained in the DIA, into which would be recorded "the name of every person who is entitled to be registered as an Indian."[17] This Indian Register continues to be maintained today (now in electronic format) in the DIA in the Indian Registration and Band Lists Directorate of the Lands and Trust Services. The Indian Register itself is part of a larger system of records that documents status and describes those vital events that affect the status of individual Indians.

A word of warning: the Indian Register is not a public register. It contains information of a highly personal nature that documents family relationships. Because its information is now maintained at the DIA in electronic format, LAC has acquired the hardcopy and microform register ledgers for the period 1951–1984 as well as annual copies from the electronic record for more recent years. However, because of the nature of the record, and because the Register continues to be operational within the DIA, there were special access conditions attached to the transfer. Indian Register data in the custody of LAC can be used for research purposes where the data are anonymized and treated collectively. However, requests for information retrieved by an individual name or identifier for the purposes of status verification, or other operational reasons, are normally referred to the DIA. Any release of personal information from Indian Register records in LAC custody can be done only in a manner consistent with the provisions of ATIP legislation.

The establishment of a centralized register in 1951 brought greater order than had previously existed to a system of recording individual-level information, and especially Indian status information, that had been functioning since the nineteenth century. Before the creation of the Register, individual-level information, including that which was used to determine status but also that which was collected primarily for other purposes, had been maintained in diverse sources most of which are represented in the holdings of RG 10, either in the form of lists or in the subject files relating to status issues.

Census Records

The national censuses that were carried out in the colonies of British North America and, later, by the federal government of Canada, up to and including the Western Census of 1906 are today available at LAC in the Statistics Canada *fonds* (RG31). These records, familiar to all genealogists, are very useful when searching for Aboriginal ancestors. Indeed, in some ways, they are of much more value than records maintained by the Indian Department in that they are full nominal censuses. On the other hand, the decennial censuses do have certain limitations for research on Indian people. First and foremost, for those interested in proving status, the census says nothing about recognized status under Indian legislation.

Also, while censuses are good for the well-established areas within the older colonies/provinces where the Indian population was more sedentary, they are incomplete for the unorganized territories within those areas and even more so for the "new" provinces that entered Confederation from 1870. Finally, since the Indian population was enumerated along with the non-Indian, they are included within the census structure of enumeration districts and sub-districts and so there are not, for the most part, obvious identifiers of Indian settlements in the census finding aids. However, it is a relatively easy matter to figure out what enumeration district includes any given reserve. Table 3 in the published census report for 1871, for example, records "origins" of the people enumerated, so it is an easy matter to check that column for concentrations of Indians in enumeration districts. Since the enumeration districts did not vary greatly from the 1851 and 1861 to the 1871 censuses, you will be able to identify the correct district for 1871 and work back to the two earlier censuses. For the purposes of this book, I did a sample trace of the Oneidas and Munceys of the Thames for 1851–1891, and there was little difficulty in locating these bands in the census records. For 1851–1881, the Indian population is easily identified since the census form in each case includes a column for (national or racial) origin. Curiously, the 1891 census was more of a problem in that the form records place of birth but not "race." The main clue here to identifying the Indian population (apart from certain obvious names) was a concentration of people recorded as having been born in Canada, an obvious distinction in a surrounding population whose place of origin was largely the British Isles. In the 1901 census, some Indian agencies are enumerated separately and those returns appear at the end of microfilm reel T-6554 and the start of reel T-6555.

The fact that the decennial census is available for genealogical research only to 1901 (along with the special 1906 Western census) makes any comment about the taking of later censuses academic. However, for anyone interested in the mechanics of census-taking, and the special circumstances surrounding the enumeration of the Aboriginal population, there is a considerable amount of correspondence in RG 10. Although the statement contained in the introduction to the published 1901 census report suggests that the use of Indian agents as enumerators for Indian communities was widespread the DIA record is more equivocal.[18] In response to a query about who was taking the census in Manitoba, DIA Secretary J. D. McLean wrote, 29 May 1901

> …the Census Commission has made no arrangement with this Department as to taking the census of the Indians, in connection with the general census being taken of the people of Canada…. I understand that for the older portions of Canada census enumerators have been instructed to include the Indian population.[19]

By the 1911 decennial census, the DIA was unquestionably cooperating with the Census and Statistics Office. Indian agents were appointed as enumerators to take the census of the Indians in their agency under the direction of the local census Commissioner. For this they received pay, as would any enumerator, over and above their DIA remuneration.[20] Similar arrangements were carried out for the 1916 census of Manitoba, Saskatchewan and Alberta and for subsequent decennial censuses up to at least 1941, the last record found.[21]

The rationale for using the Indian agents was obvious. They knew the population and represented the authority figure on the reserve who was more likely to get cooperation than would a stranger. Indeed, in some isolated areas the Indian agent also acted as enumerator for the non-Indian population, being one of the few government officers available. The records do reveal interesting differences in perspective on the Aboriginal population as seen by the DIA and the Dominion Bureau of Statistics (DBS), the question of status being the most obvious.[22] They also show that, despite all the good intentions in enlisting Indian agents to ensure the compliance of the Indians, even that did not ensure cooperation. There are a number of reported incidents of Indians refusing to be enumerated. In the face of the refusal of the Roseau Rapids band to cooperate in 1916 the DIA obtained a legal opinion that concluded that nothing in the Indian Act could force compliance.[23] In 1931, people at Oka, St.Regis, Brantford and Rocky Mountain House refused to cooperate with "the white man's law." The DIA, for its part, stood to its position that nothing in the Indian Act could be used to compel compliance and recommended the DBS use the powers of its own legislation, which it did by charging the offenders.[24]

"Indian Censuses"

In addition to these national censuses there are a number of records that were created by the DIA in its efforts to record the Indian population. For example, lists of Indians, more frequently than not with only heads of family specifically named, were created during the pre-Confederation period and are found scattered in RG 10 records from that era. They may be referred to in the finding aids as "censuses" even though the records were not created for the express purpose of counting Indians but for other transactions such as documenting the distribution of presents or money.[25]

Moreover, from 1871 to 1917, the DIA did take its own "Indian census" annually. The clientele department needed accurate statistics on the size of its client; on such figures the expenditure of money and the direction of policy depended.[26] The band population figures that appear in the published DIA *Annual Report* up to 1916 are summaries drawn from these annual censuses. These were aggregate censuses for each band; nominal returns were not required. The following instructions, contained in an 1886 circular despatched to agents in Eastern Canada, describe the process. The agent was advised that the following spring he was

> to take a careful Census of the band or bands of Indians within your District, and to make a return thereof on the form of which a supply is transmitted herewith. Only those who properly and legally belong to the band or bands under your charge should be included in the Return and a separate Return on the same form should be made of any Indians who hang about, or reside upon, or in the vicinity of, the Reserve, but who are not members of the band owning the same, and full particulars in respect to each such Indian should be given.
>
> On reserves where Annuity or other moneys are paid periodically the Census should be taken once a year at the time of such payments, and the number of Indians on the Pay Sheets should correspond with the Census Return of the members of the band.[27]

There are a number of files scattered through both the headquarters central registry Red and Black series that contain correspondence about the taking of the annual census with queries from individual agents on the finer points of gathering the required statistics. Many of these files include aggregate band population returns but only occasionally do they include anything of more detail. Nevertheless, the indexes of these series should be checked for possible references.[28]

In 1917, the DIA decided to dispense with the gathering of census statistics on an annual basis and move to a quinquennial census. This was not, in fact, carried into effect until 1923, the disruption of World War I and its aftermath doubtless a contributing factor in the delay. An Indian census was taken in that year and the band aggregate information published in 1924. These quinquennial censuses continued to be taken and their results published until 1959. Although agents were expected to send only aggregate data to Ottawa for the purposes of this publication, a circular issued in 1939 makes the point clear that they were also expected to keep a full nominal roll in their agency office:

> When taking the census records you should make an accurate list showing the names, sex, age, and civil status … and band number of every Indian in your agency and keep it in your office …. All Indians who are on the paylist of a band or where there is no paylist, reputed to be members of the band whether on reserve or not should be included in this census…[29]

Unfortunately, many of the detailed census records that were retained in agency offices either have not survived or have yet to be transferred to LAC custody. RG 10 does include a series containing a few "census" records (as distinct from those censuses found in files). Included are scattered returns for selected years with varying degrees of detail (some fully nominal) for southwestern Ontario; the Robinson Huron and Superior treaty areas; the Montagnais bands of Quebec; Rolling River Band (Manitoba); Duck Lake and Onion Lake agencies in Saskatchewan; and a number of British Columbia bands. As well, volumes 12608–12610 contain a collection of British Columbia agency census books from the Babine, Kamloops, Kootenay, Thompson, Lytton, Nicola and Okanagan agencies. However, because of the poor survival rate of field office records with the amalgamation/closure of offices that have been going on since the 1960s, it seems likely that other such records are largely lost although some may yet appear, particularly in transfers from DIA District or Regional offices to LAC regional records centres. For the period after 1951 the Indian Register, of course, is as complete a record of individuals as exists. However, for the pre-1951 period, such census records would be an extremely valuable research tool.

Vital Statistics Records

"Vital Stats" — the Recording Of Births, Marriages and Deaths

The search for vital records (births, marriages, deaths) for individual status Indians should begin, depending upon the time period under scrutiny, not in RG 10 but in those sources familiar to all genealogists, the vital statistics records maintained by the provinces and the individual churches. For Indian genealogy, the basic problems with provincial civil registration records — varying degrees of completeness from jurisdiction to jurisdiction and the relatively limited time period for which the records exist — are compounded by the unique position of Indians vis-a-vis provincial authorities. Indians are a federal responsibility and civil registration is a provincial one and there is evidence of some confusion on the part of both the provincial and federal authorities as to their responsibilities for the registration of Indian vital statistics.

Responsibility for Collecting Indian Vital Records

As early as 1885 the DIA received a legal opinion from the Department of Justice that provincial legislation (in this instance, that of Ontario and Quebec) respecting the registration of births, marriages and deaths should be complied with by Indians on reserves wherever the law was in force. Unfortunately, the file containing this opinion does not address the question of responsibility for compliance — whether it was individual or departmental. The wording of the opinion leaves the impression that responsibility lay not with a DIA officer but with the individual Indian or clergy or doctor (depending upon the circumstances) attending the event.[30] Yet, for a later period, we know from other records that a regular system of supplying information to the provincial authorities, in the case of Ontario at least, was in place. The Circular to nine Ontario agents, dated 5 March 1917, asks whether they had complied with the request of the provincial government to furnish birth/marriage/death statistics for their agency for 1916. A general circular with, unfortunately, no indication of the specific agents to whom it was sent or even the province to which it was to apply, was sent out 28 February 1919 advising the recipients that the DIA had been advised that no regular returns had been made to the provincial registrar and reminding them that this "is considered to be a part of your official duties, and neglect of performance will not be overlooked." Moreover, the agents were especially instructed to enlist the aid of the missionaries to ensure receipt of notice of marriages performed and that of the local doctors to ensure timely dispatch to the agent of death notification.[31]

The situation varied from province to province. Early in 1914, the Deputy Registrar General of

Alberta advised the DIA that, up to that point, his office had registered no Indian births or deaths and requested an opinion as to whether there was any good reason why Indians should not be included in that province's vital statistics records. After obtaining a legal opinion (which said that there seemed to be no reason why the provincial law should not be made operative for Indians) the DIA put the matter of data collection firmly back into provincial hands with the reply that

> there is no provision in our Indian Act whereby the Provincial laws in this matter can be made applicable. The Department, however, sees no reason why your Act should not apply to Indians as well as Whites and would be glad if you would endeavour to have it enforced with respect to Indians.[32]

A list of names and addresses of local Indian agents was subsequently provided although there is nothing in the file to suggest that these agents were themselves instructed to provide the statistics. Six years later the problem had not been solved. In January 1920, the Acting Deputy Registrar of Alberta advised the DIA of the "considerable trouble" experienced in extending the requirements of the Vital Statistics Act to Indian reserves, noting that "the registration of births, marriages and deaths are not received from these reserves in anything approaching completeness. The difficulty so far has been the appointment of Registrars." Again the DIA response was to suggest that contact be made with the local Indian agents.[33]

The depth of the provincial confusion is illustrated further by a letter received at the DIA from the official provincial registrar from North Battleford, Saskatchewan, 11 March 1920, in which he enclosed the registration papers relating to a recent Indian death with the comment that he understood that Indian vital statistics were not registered by the province "but are entirely handled by your Department."

The DIA received a legal opinion four years later in response to the request of a missionary seeking to know what was required of him in reporting the baptisms, marriages and deaths with which he dealt and whether the "usual" practice of advising the local Indian agent was sufficient. In his reply the Departmental solicitor was unequivocal in stating that the provisions of the Vital Statistics Act should be observed and the reports required under that legislation should be made to whatever person the Act required. He was doubtless close to the truth in his comment about the confusion in practice, however, observing that the "prevailing notion that Provincial law does not apply to the Indians or… perhaps indifference on the part of the Provincial authorities" lay at the root of the problem.

In British Columbia, on the other hand, the situation was handled differently. There neither the provincial nor the federal authorities wanted to take the responsibility, each arguing that the other's legislation should be amended to ensure that Indian vital statistics were recorded. After considerable debate, a modus operandi was achieved in which the provincial vital statistics act that had, heretofore, specifically excluded Indians from registration was amended in 1916 and the DIA Indian agents appointed as district registrars of births and deaths under the Vital Statistics Act and also registrars under the Marriage Act. In both cases their jurisdiction extended only to their Indian charges. They were to take their instructions from the provincial authorities and report on registration matters directly to the provincial Registrar's office.[34] By giving the Indian agent an official capacity under the provincial legislation, of course, he was thus made a vital link in both the process and the information chain. As an official of provincial registration under the Marriage Act, it was the agent to whom the missionaries were required to provide data about marriages. Furthermore, the Indian agent was himself appointed Marriage Registrar (later Marriage Commissioner) for Indians only under the provincial Marriage Act.

This empowered him to issue marriage licences, to solemnize religious marriages and to, himself, solemnize marriages by civil contract. As deputy (later district) registrar of vital statistics it was the agent to whom local physicians now reported Indian deaths.

Indian agents acting for the province

From the evidence uncovered for this book it would seem that the practice was largely established before 1930 that Indian agents acted as agents of the provincial government for vital statistics registration purposes.[35] The fact that a DIA officer took on registration duties at least filled a vacuum such as that which had existed in British Columbia. However, it still remained true that the thoroughness of the work was greatly dependent upon the degree of contact between the Indian agent and his charges and the availability to the agent of other sources of information, such as missionaries. It remained the case in more isolated areas or with nomadic bands that the agent might see his charges only once or twice a year if at all. Even where the will existed and policy demanded compliance, civil registration was not a guaranteed thing.

And, moreover, the record that was created as a result of a federal Indian agent performing duties for the provincial government did not as a matter of course end up in the permanent record of the Indian Department. Indeed, there are relatively few cases where the agents' copies of such provincial civil registration records have survived to find their way into RG 10.

Filling the Civil Registration Gaps

If the records of provincial civil registration are flawed by virtue of the circumstances described above, to what extent do DIA records fill the gaps? The fact that the DIA — in some parts of the country at least — did not, through its agents, formally take on the role of reporting vital statistics to the provincial authorities until well after provincial vital statistics legislation was in effect for the population-at-large, did not mean that a record of those events was not being maintained in some form by the DIA for its own purposes. Indeed, the local agent had to keep just such a record in order to keep track of his charges. As has been mentioned already, an agency nominal roll or census record was formally maintained in agency offices from at least the 1930s.[36] In treaty areas, the annuity paylists recorded numbers of births and deaths in each family as was required in order to determine correct per capita payments.

Paylists

Paylists are probably the most widely known of the DIA records used by the genealogist. They are key records for certain types of research yet frustratingly inadequate for others.[37] Although their post-1951 utility as a genealogical resource has been greatly reduced by the presence of the Indian Register, they remain an important record for the pre-1951 period. They are currently open for research up to 31 December 1909; more recent paylists can be consulted only in a manner consistent with the provisions of the Privacy Act.

Basically, there are two types of lists. For those treaty Indians to whom yearly payments (annuities) are made in accordance with the terms of a treaty, there are "treaty annuity paylists." [See the illustration opposite.] The Indian Act, historically, made provision also for the periodic distribution to band members of per capita shares from band monies held in trust. Lists known as "interest distribution paylists" were created for documenting this payment. The historical format of both types of list is similar.

Pay List of Robinson Treaty Annuities.

157940

Garden River Ojibway **Band.**

Paid at Garden River, Sault Ste. Marie & Lake Superior, 189 4

Band No.	NAMES.	Men.	Women	Boys.	Girls.	Number Paid.	Amount.	Number paid last year.	DECREASE. By Death.	By Emigration.	INCREASE. By Emigration.	By Birth.	SIGNATURE.	REMARKS.
1	Medore Augustin	1				1	4 00	1					Medore Abbott enrolled on ₤ of Chippin	
2	Chief Pequakchene			2	2	5	32 00	5					x Self	
3	Charles Kanonaud	1	1			1	4 00	1					x Self	
5	Mille Shore	1	1		1	4	12 00	3					x Self	
6	Joe Shward	2	2			4	16 00	4					x Self	
7	Members James Kerre	1	1			2	8 00	2					Re enter 12 Oct P.C Aug 479	
8	Daniel Kernige 2d	1			1	2	4 00	1					x Sen.	
9	James Muniyyai	3	2			5	20 00	5					x enrolled many children 2d August P.C Aug 98 see also no 12	
11	James Pines Jame.			1	1	2	8 00	2					x Self	
12	Michel Bachette	3	4	1	1	9	36 00	9					x Self	
13	Askin	2	1	1	1	5	20 00	5					x Self	
14	Joe Liuage	2	2	5		9	36 00	9					x Self	
15	Jabo Boulonnais	2	5			7	28 00	6					x Self	
16	Joe Pino	1	2			6	24 00	6					x Self	
17	Michel Bellomo	2	2	2	1	7	28 00	7					x Self	
18	Nahonmoan	1	1			2	8 00	2					x Self	
19	Jacob Thompson	1	1			2	8 00	2					x Self	
20	Wawshawgogis	2	1	1		4	16 00	4					x Medow	
21	Frank Clark	4	5		3	13	52 00	13					x Self	
23	Joe Pino Jam	1	1			2	8 00	2					x Self	
25	John Augustin	3	1	1	3	7	28 00						x Self	
26	Charles Pino	4	1	1	1	9	36 00	9					x Self	
27	John Wigwass	2	2	2		6	24 00	6					x Self	
28	Mahgahwahnedow	1	1	2	1	7	28 00	6					x Self	
29	Petor Jones	2	1			5	20 00	5					x Self	
30	Emmeline Payjemo	2	2		2	6	24 00	6					x Self	
	Carried forward	57	45	25	22	127	576 00	129						130

Form No. 78.

Paylist of Robinson Treaty Annuities - Garden River Band. Paid at Garden River, Sault Ste. Marie & Lake Superior, 1894/Library and Archives Canada/C-92648

The Headquarters Copy

Although researchers tend to consider the headquarters copy as the definitive paylist, they overlook the fact that three copies were generated. Two were sent to headquarters and one retained in the agency. It was this copy that the agent often used as his working document to record changes to band make-up during the year before the next payment. Researchers, who have bothered to look, have found discrepancies in the information on the various copies, so where copies other than the headquarters one exist, it is a good idea to check them. The problem is that, as with all field office records, the agency copies have frequently not survived.

Because they were created to document the payment of money to eligible Indians, there was no need for paylists to record the names of every family member. All that was required was that the amount of payment to each household be kept accurately. So, many of the earliest paylists provide names for only the head of the household. In such cases the numbers of other family members are recorded in separate columns for men, women, boys, girls and other relatives. In addition, the lists record births and deaths that occurred in each household since the previous payment and indicate whether these were, as appropriate, men, women, boys or girls. Other movements into or out of the household are also noted, such as enfranchisements, transfers from, or to, other bands (with the bands identified) or transfers to other households within the band. Boys, upon reaching the age of majority, were usually entered separately under their own names and numbers on the lists, as were women who married non-Indians but did not commute their annuities. A "remarks" column permitted the recording of any details relevant to the entries and the notations, here, can be very useful in explaining family relationships and individual movements. For later years, it is not uncommon to find references noted here to the files that explain the event recorded on the paylist.

The Limitation of Paylists

The limitations of such lists are obvious. Treaty annuity paylists exist only for those Indians belonging to a treaty and are thus limited to the bands of the Robinson Huron and Superior treaties, Treaty 9, and the Cayuga in Ontario, and the numbered western treaties. Obviously, they date only from the treaty signing. The gaps left for eastern Canada and most of British Columbia are filled somewhat by the interest distribution paylists, the earliest of which (in the main series at least) date from 1856 only. Not all bands had the resources to generate interest in their trust fund account, however, and so a distribution may not have been possible or, when it was, it occurred irregularly. There are a number of bands for which neither type of paylist exists.

Even where there is a paylist, its utility as a genealogical source has further limitations. A woman can be born and — after living a full life — die, and never be named on the paylist. Moreover, the inclusion of an ancestor's name on a paylist is not, in itself, proof of status for either the ancestor or the descendants. There are cases in which people were enrolled in treaty and their names entered on paylists, but who subsequently withdrew from treaty (for example, to take scrip) or who, upon investigation — sometimes many years later — had their status taken away by the DIA. Prior to 1951, women who married non-Indians lost their status but were still entitled to share in treaty distributions. Unless they took their share of money in a lump sum (commuted their annuity), they could continue to draw annual payments and so their names remained on the lists. These women were supposed to be identified on the paylists but not all agents were meticulous in this. Such situations only underline the fact that these records must frequently be used in conjunction with the other documentation — usually files that explain the events recorded on the lists.

Documenting the Payment Process

The various sub-series that make up the Headquarters central registry system series within RG 10 all contain records that document the payment process itself. These often take the form of correspondence between headquarters and the field about the arrangements for payments of both treaty and interest and any discrepancies in the lists produced. They may include the paying officer's report of the distribution and some include copies of the paylists.[38] Depending upon the personal information found in them, these files may be open, or restricted and subject to review under ATIP before the release of information. File access status is indicated in the finding aids. As with many other of the holdings of RG 10, files relating to payments may also be found in field office records.

Membership/Status Records

Checking band membership or status

A variety of files contained in separate classification blocks, now found in the RG 10 Headquarters central registry system series, document specific changes in band/family composition, some of which also involve changes in Indian status. There are separate file blocks for "enfranchisements" (the voluntary or involuntary loss of Indian status, originally symbolized by the taking of the franchise) and for "commutations," in addition to blocks designated as "membership" files that are devoted to all aspects of status and band membership.

As a general rule, the membership and commutation files were created on an agency basis, with the result that the correspondence relating to any individual event will be filed with that of all other similar events for all bands throughout an agency.[39] Enfranchisement records, on the other hand, can take the form of individual case files, with the finding aids indicating the name of the individual referred to in each file.[40] As with other types of records, field office holdings will also include membership/status files and miscellaneous records that should be compared with the headquarters documents.[41]

Other Miscellaneous Records

In addition to the records relating to membership and status that are found in the Headquarters central registry system series, there are also scattered miscellaneous records from both headquarters and field offices that may, depending on the individual research question, be relevant. For example, in setting up the Indian Register in 1951, the DIA had first to establish a base list of who would be included. Individual lists were drawn up for each band and posted in the relevant community; a period was provided in which protests could be entered concerning the eligibility of individuals listed. The "band membership posted lists" are found in RG 10, vols. 11582–11586. Entries on each list are organized by band number and the lists provide names for everyone, but no additional information. A small selection of files relating to protests launched in individual cases is also available.[42] A small number of membership registers and lists, varying in format and detail of information, exist among the RG 10 headquarters miscellaneous holdings for select Ontario, Prairie and British Columbia bands (for example, Six Nations covering the years 1902–1935).[43] Such records will also be found scattered among the field office holdings. See, for example, the membership and status investigation records for a number of British Columbia agencies, some with individual data dating to the 1890s, in the records of the Office of the Indian Commissioner for British Columbia found in RG 10, vols. 11294-11295. Because of the personal nature of the content of these records, they are almost invariably subject to review under the Privacy Act before any information can be made available. A small number of policy files for the subjects discussed are open. There are also anomalies. For example, although the detailed enfranchise-

Statement of Enfranchisements under the Indian
Act, from the first day of the fiscal year beginning
April 1, 1921, to March 9, 1922, for submission to both
Houses of Parliament, as required by Section 111 of the
said Act.

Note: The names appear in chronological order.

Name	Band	Section of Indian Act
Mrs. Rose Miron	Garden River	122A.
Charles Miron Ellen Driver Miron Mary Irene Miron Norah Mae Miron Blanche Elizabeth Miron	Garden River	122A.
Joseph Thos. Miron Irene Marie Miron	Garden River	122A
James Jacques Loukes Jean Loukes Gerald Ross Loukes Lois Jean Loukes	Mississaugas of Alnwick	122A
James Johnsons Martha Johnson	Mississaugas of The Credit	122A.
Marguerite Olive Wood	Mississaugas of the Credit	122A
Zimmer E. Noah	Moravians of the Thames	122A
Joseph Powless Ina Powless Marion Powless	Six Nations	122A
James Gordon Sherry	Six Nations	122A
Arthur L. Smith	Six Nations	122A
Charles Jamieson Clara Jamieson Melvyn Russell Jamieson	Six Nations	122A
William Cook Emily Elizabeth Cook	Nimkish	122A
Lula Maracle	Mohawks of the Bay of Quinte	122A
Freeman Lewis	Moravians of the Thames	122A
Ignatius Singleton	Fort William	122A
Essie Eve Claus	Mohawks of the Bay of Quinte	122A
Geo. F. Singleton Jessie M. Collins Singleton David Clifford Singleton	Fort William	122A
Peter Belanger	Fort William	122A

Extract from a statement of enfranchisement under the Indian Act from … April 1, 1921 to March 9, 1922.
Such lists were submitted to Parliament as required by Section 111/Library and Archives Canada/C-142523

ment records themselves are subject to review under ATIP, lists of those enfranchised for the period 1920–1945 are fully open without restriction in RG 10, vol. 2876, file 177066, parts 1 and 2 [see Illustration No.4 on p. 33]. It was a requirement that such lists be provided annually to Parliament and it is copies of those lists that are found in this file.

Individual Records of Economic Activity

As with so many other records discussed here, it holds true that until the relatively recent introduction of individual case files into the DIA records-keeping system, most evidence of individual economic activity will be found scattered throughout general agency or band files in the relevant subject areas. Farming records are a case in point. DIA policy historically put a great emphasis on the need to create successful Indian farmers. There is a considerable amount of documentary material in the Black Series headquarters files, and in the agency records for the West in the late-nineteenth and early twentieth centuries, that relates to agricultural development. However, in order to find reference to specific Indian farmers you must go through such records as agents' narrative and statistical reports in the hope that a particularly successful individual will be identified.

The same is largely true of the records that document other types of resource exploitation by Indians. There is a sizeable block of records relating to fur, game and trapping in the RG 10 Headquarters central registry system series, but these are policy, general and project files. Although these contain such things as lists of trappers operating in an area, and discussion of individual cases that may have warranted special note, essentially, they are not "individual" files. In the case of trapping records there are, fortunately, small pockets of very valuable case files of trapline registration that even include maps of individual Indians' traplines, but these are the exception and are largely restricted to areas in British Columbia.[44]

Loans and Grant Files

Some measure of individual-level economic activity exists in loans and grants files. The 1927 Indian Act sanctioned the creation of a "revolving fund" from which money from the Consolidated Revenue could be used to promote band, group and individual economic development projects, including such things as the purchase of machinery and livestock. Applications for loans from this fund date from 1939, with those from the late 1940s and 1950s providing the most detailed information on individual borrowers (for example, name, age, occupation, dependants, income, description of land and chattels, terms of loan, agent's recommendation on the suitability of the applicant). Besides the application records, there is also a series of individual case files, identified by name of borrower, that document both the application and the loan repayment process.[45]

It was from this program that the Indian Economic Development Fund program of loans and grants developed. Both general files, which will include references to individuals, and case files exist. Of the latter which are found in RG 10, they are concentrated largely in field office holdings, both regional and agency/district. Many of these are not yet fully processed and a significant proportion of them are held in LAC custody in regional records centres and not in Ottawa.[46]

Loans from band funds files

Similarly, records of loans from band funds are also found in RG 10. A block of band loan records,[47] although primarily accounting records of loan repayments, does provide some information on the borrower's economic situation. These records exist for a small number of bands only. A larger series of case files, most from the twentieth century but some dating back to the nineteenth, is found in the

Headquarters central registry system series.[48] These records are organized by agency but each file title includes the individual borrower's name.

Social Records

Indian Health Records

In the "social records" category I include those records of social assistance, community development and social control for which there is individual-level information. There are relatively few records of Indian health in RG 10. With the transfer of responsibility for the delivery of health care to Indians from the DIA to the Department of National Health and Welfare in 1945, much of the record went too. In fact, it is only recently that the LAC has received a major transfer of Indian Health Service files from the Medical Services Branch of that department; these records are maintained in the Medical Services Branch *sous-fonds*, Central registry files series in RG 29. This is not to say that there are no records of health services to Indians in RG 10, but what there is tends to be policy and general files, or correspondence concerning the employment of doctors and payment of their accounts from the late-nineteenth and early twentieth centuries rather than records in which individual Indians are identified. That said, a fascinating, if small, series of British Columbia hospital records came to light in an accession of material transferred to LAC custody at the Pacific Region Federal Records Centre in Vancouver. In these are returns of patients treated at the Port Simpson and Port Essington hospitals from 1903 to 1939. Included is such information as patient name, gender, residence, age, band, admission and discharge dates, disease and treatment. Access to these records is subject to review under ATIP prior to release of information.[49]

Within the DIA Headquarters central registry files series in RG 10 are file blocks devoted to a range of "social" subjects such as Indian housing,[50] general welfare, funerals; and child care,[51] and welfare equipment and supplies.[52] In none of these records are there specific case files although, as with so much from the DIA filing system, "general" files include a great deal relating to individual cases.[53] Case files for these subjects will be found in the field office records, both at the regional and agency/district level, many of which are in LAC custody at regional records centres. In addition, surviving in a few RG 10 field office accessions are what were known as "Personal" files. As late as the mid-1960s, DIA records manuals were still recommending the creation of omnibus personal files in which were to be placed all records relating to an individual regardless of the subject of correspondence. This system was later changed and individual case files created according to subject. Given the scattered occurrence of the "Personal" files among records transferred to LAC custody, it would seem that the "Personal" files must have been largely broken up and their contents dispersed to appropriate subject file blocks.

Law Enforcement Records

Another example within the category "social records" are records of social control and, in particular, law enforcement. Files relating to individual transgressions of the law will be found scattered throughout the Red and Black series of headquarters central registry records, usually identified by name of offender and/or victim. The Headquarters central registry system series includes a block of twentieth-century murder case files that are virtually all open.[54] Content varies greatly from file to file but may include agents' reports, press cuttings, correspondence relating to legal counsel, police reports and detailed trial transcripts. The Headquarters central registry system series also includes a small scattering of records relating to various law enforcement subjects as set out in the DIA classification (for example, accidents, truancy, juvenile delinquency). These are general, not case files.[55] Similar records created at the regional and agency/district level will be found in field office records in LAC custody both in Ottawa and in the regional record centres.

Education Records

Indian Education and Schools

No single subject, with the exception of land, is more extensively documented in RG 10 than is education and schools. Records that identify individual pupils are varied; they are found in the Headquarters central registry system series, in miscellaneous headquarters records series and in field office holdings throughout RG 10. A copy of the DIAND Indian Education Nominal Roll electronic records system for the period 1970–1980 is included in the holdings. Records relating to Indian teachers, such as applications to teach, will be found in the same sources cited later for non-Indian teachers.

As with most records of DIA administration for the post-Confederation period, the search in RG 10 for individual-level information about Indian students is best started in the Headquarters central registry system series. Individual student case files are not found in this large series.

There are a great number of general administration files for both day and residential schools, identified in the finding aids by name of school or agency. Such files contain a considerable amount of individual-level information.[56] There are also subject-specific files that provide particular personal data, such as files on deaths of pupils in school, admissions and discharges, and monthly/quarterly returns for schools. Admissions and discharges files for individual schools, for example, contain "Application for Admission" forms that, although they vary over the years, include pupil name, birth date, band and number, previous school, grade, parents' names, religion, agents' recommendation and results of medical examinations. Although there are also quarterly returns of admissions and discharges (giving name, date of admission and discharge, parents' names and level achieved), discharges tend also to be documented through correspondence, especially if the discharge is the result of misbehaviour. In the case of truants and runaways, the file may contain police reports.[57]

Reports Submitted by the Principals

Quarterly returns files, on the other hand, contain the record of continuing attendance at residential schools throughout the school year. Since grants for school operation were based upon numbers in attendance, it was important that a careful record be kept. The quarterly returns submitted by the school principal record pupil name, gender, birth date, band number, grade enrolled, class of study and number of days resident.[58]

Another series of records available for many schools is the Principal's Monthly Reports (PMRs). These are not primarily nominal records; rather the principal reported aggregate attendance figures and grade distribution. However, the standard report form that came into use in the early 1950s did require explanation for absentees and so names of these and details of cause are routinely included.[59]

The operation of the education system is also reflected extensively in field office records now in LAC custody both at Ottawa and in the regional record centres. With education being one of the first services to be decentralized by the DIA, the appearance of such records in the regional record centres has increased over the past two decades. Field office records transferred to the LAC frequently include educational assistance case files, but also such records as applications for admission to schools, discharge documentation, quarterly returns, school inspection reports and correspondence on all aspects of school administration. Unfortunately, only very rarely are found the "permanent school record" files that were created to document each individual student's passage through the education system.[60]

QUARTERLY SCHOOL RETURN

NOTE—READ CAREFULLY AND COMPLY WITH "INSTRUCTIONS TO TEACHERS" ON FRONT OF THIS FORM

Quarterly school return, Carmacks and Ross River School, Yukon Territory, 1925. Such records show name, age, gender, band affiliation, class standing and attendance/Library and Archives Canada/C-142522

Individual Reserve Land Possession and Property Records

Land Allocation on Indian Reserves

The Indian Land Registry in DIAND, which will be discussed further in the section dealing with land transactions involving non-Indians, is the best source for records of the allocation of land on reserve. However, there are also records found throughout the Headquarters central registry system series that relate to the allocation of parcels of reserve land — known historically as "locations" — to individual band members. The finding aids to those series should be checked for the appropriate agency and reserve. Some references will also be found under the name of the occupant, particularly if a dispute was involved and a file generated to document it.

The system of reserve land allocation is complicated. Individuals do not "own" reserve land in fee simple. Prior to the 1951 Indian Act, band members obtained certain rights to occupy, use and pass on to their status heirs parcels of reserve land (or locations) recognized as being designated theirs. The records that served as proof of this right to use, and occupy, the land were known as "location tickets." The 1951 Indian Act amended the system, and location tickets were replaced by certificates of possession, certificates of occupation or notices of entitlement.[61] Registers of location tickets for a number of reserves are found in RG 10, vols. 11896–11923 and 11971–2. Some date back to the nineteenth century. The more recent ones describe each parcel of land in a reserve, indicate the date and nature of the instrument being recorded (transfer, sale, agreement, ministerial order, inheritance), name and band of the grantee, devisee and information concerning the type of certificate issued. There is also a block of location ticket general and case files in the Headquarters central registry system series (RG 10, vols. 7616–7623), as illustrated on page 34. The complicated issue of the land occupation of the Caughnawaga reserve is particularly well-documented with RG 10 including both W. M. Walbank's reference books for his 1885 subdivision (RG 10, vols. 8968–8972) and Commissioner C. H. Taggert's 1947–1948 up-date of that record (RG 10, vols. 12028–12029).

Deceased Indian Estates Administration

The administration of the estates of deceased Indians is also extensively documented in RG 10. Rules governing the descent of Indian property were introduced in An Act for the Gradual Enfranchisement of Indians… in 1869, and consolidated in the Indian Act of 1876.[62] Successive acts and the regulations passed under their authority refined the rules governing estates distribution. Although legislation passed in 1894 made provision specifically for Indians, under certain conditions, to avail themselves of the same facilities for estate administration as were available to non-Indians, many Indians continued to opt for the service provided by the DIA and continue to do so today. For those people, then, the estates functions performed by DIAND are the equivalent of those available to the non-Indian community through legal representatives and the provinces: probate, appointment of personal representatives, securing assets and, where the individual dies intestate, determining heirs, verifying and paying debts and distributing assets.

The estates function within the DIA has been largely devolved to the field office level for some time. It is at the Regional and District offices that the actual administration of the estate takes place. Estates case files are found scattered throughout many accessions of records that have been transferred from those offices to LAC custody, especially at the regional record centres.

Those estates files that will be found in RG 10 holdings in Ottawa date from the period prior to regionalization, largely from the 1940s and 1950s. A large number are found in the Headquarters cen-

Form C.

INDIAN LOCATION TICKET

Issued under Section 15 Indian Act

DUPLICATE FOR AGENT.

Be it Known by these Presents *that*

Daniel Albert

of the Caradoc — — — — — — — *Indian Reserve*
in the Township of Caradoc
in the County *of* Middlesex
in the Province of Ontario

and Dominion of Canada, being a member of the Chippewas
of the Thames Band of Indians —
*having been allotted by the Band owning the Reserve, with the approval
of the Superintendent General, the* North part of South Half
of Lot One. Range Five —

on the aforesaid Reserve, containing by admeasurement Thirty
three — — — *acres of land, more or less, is hereby located
for the same, under the provisions of Sections* 16 · 17 *and* 18 *of the
Indian Act, Chap.* 43, *Revised Statutes of Canada.*

Given under my Hand and Seal at Ottawa, this Sixteenth *day
of* May — — — — *in the year of Our Lord, one thousand nine
hundred and* Four.

DEPUTY SUPERINTENDENT GENERAL OF INDIAN AFFAIRS.

*Indian Location Ticket issued to Daniel Albert, Chippewas of the Thames Band, for the North part of the
South half of Lot one, Range five, Caradoc Reserve, 16 May 1904/Library and Archives Canada/C-142517*

tral registry system series microform case files records (RG 10, reels M-2521–2777), all of which are subject to review under ATIP prior to release of information. Another number are found among the Maritime field office records in RG 10, vols. 8324–8386.

The Size of the Estate File

The content of any estate file varies with the complexity of the case, so it is difficult to generalize. However, the following DIA forms appear frequently on the microform case files mentioned above: "Notice to Creditors," "Application for Administration or Probate," "Application for Appointment of Administrator and Approval of Will," "Succession Duties — Statement of Value and Relationship" and "Investigators Progress Report on Estate." These forms record tombstone data on the deceased; summaries of land assets and of personal assets with values of chattels, property and monies held; summaries of debts; lists of heirs at law and/or next of kin (with tombstone data on them).

What Is in Estates Administration Files?

Other DIA forms and documents might appear on the files, as the case warrants. These include "Transfer of Land by Administrator" form; "Quit Claim of Rights to Land in an Indian Reserve" form; "Appointment of Guardian" form for those deceased survived by children; copies of last will and testament of the deceased (although many died intestate); affidavits and statutory declarations made out by interested parties; maps (where land is involved); genealogical documentation (where tracing heirs is involved); copies of police reports concerning circumstances of death; funeral bills; documentation and medical certificates in cases where the deceased was mentally incompetent and in a private or public mental institution; financial information concerning any estate account and the dispersal of its contents; copies of Band Council Resolutions; correspondence between the local Indian Superintendent and the Administrator of Estates at DIA HQ, with provincial authorities, with lawyers, and with DIA's legal advisors concerning the estate.

Military Records

Reference was made earlier to the military aspect of the Indian/government relationship from before the creation of the office of Superintendent of Indian Affairs in 1755 until the end of hostilities in 1814. There is a long and proud tradition of Indian people bearing arms in support of, first, their British and, later, their Canadian allies. The records of primary value for a search of individual Indian warriors from the colonial period are not found in RG 10, but rather scattered in the extensive series of Indian papers in RG 8 (British Military and Naval Records), vols. 247–271, and in the private manuscript collections of the period — the Haldimand Papers in the British Library (copies in MG 21 at the LAC) and the Claus Papers in the LAC (MG 19, F1) being examples. As regards the War of 1812, there are a few scattered documents of interest in RG 10 for those tracing individuals. RG 10, vol. 715, for example, includes a record of Indian claimants, in what is now southwestern Ontario, for losses suffered. The ledger includes name of claimant and items for which compensation is claimed. Included, as well, are correspondence and some claims petitions with memoranda of decisions of the Board of Claims. Equally interesting is a file of correspondence dating from 1879-1948 and relating to pensions for Indian veterans of the War of 1812. Individuals are named, although they were few in number by 1875, when surviving veterans were awarded a $20 per annum pension.[63]

Anyone who has traced an Indian combatant in one of the two world wars of the twentieth century will already be aware of the military personnel case files held at LAC. The personnel case files of those who enlisted in the Canadian Expeditionary Force during the First World War are open to unrestricted

Privates David Lands (Eagle Lake), Philip Pelly (Grassy Narrows) and William Semia (Cat Lake) [left to right], c.1918/Library and Archives Canada/ C-118613

INDIAN AGENT'S OFFICE

_____ 191

IN YOUR REPLY REFER TO
No. _____
ALSO
TO DATE OF THIS LETTER

Sir,—

on his arrival in Canada in December 1918 he could speak English as well as print addresses.

He was delighted with his trip and well satisfied with the treatment received

His experiences as told in his own words were as follows:-

When me first heard about the war me want to go but my father he say "No". But in 1916 me see Indian from Nipigon with tourist. Me tell him me want to go out and be soldier. He say "alright come with us". Then my father he say "alright" too but the "Chief" come to me and say me hear you go away to the war. Me say "Yes". He says "you stay right here that war no place for injuns. Me say "alright" but just the same me go to war that very night.

Me come to Fort Arthur and join "Bull Moose" Battalion. Me like to be soldier. Lots to eat and plenty clothes. Port Arthur fine town with street cars, big boats and picture show.

Me go across ocean on "Olympic" This big boat but me sick all time on water. Me like England fine. Lots of

Extract of a report of the war experiences of Private William Semia, 52nd Battalion, as told to the local Indian agent/ Library and Archives Canada/C-142519

research and are found in the Ministry of the Overseas Military Forces of Canada *fonds* (RG 150). A database titled *Soldiers of the First World War*, available on the LAC Web site <www.collectionscanada.ca>, provides references to the case files as well as digitized images of the attestation papers (the forms signed by all those who enlisted for overseas service) of some of the soldiers. These attestation papers are one of a number of documents normally found on a military personnel case file. Other documents may include a record of discharge, military units served with and, in some cases, information concerning medical history or medals awarded.

Military personnel case files dating after 1918, on the other hand, are not open for unrestricted research and there is no on-line database for these records. Varying types of information contained in these files may be released under certain circumstances. Those interested in consulting a post-1918 military personnel case file should first review the information and instructions provided on the LAC's Canadian Genealogy Centre Web site <www.genealogy.gc.ca> — select Sources by Topic, then Military, then Canadian Forces After 1918 — and then contact the Personnel Records Unit with the information and documentation required.

Natives Who Fought in the World Wars

Indian participation in both world wars is also documented extensively in RG 10. The most complete study available for Indian service in World Wars I and II is *Forgotten Soldiers: An Illustrated History of Canada's Native Peoples in Both World Wars* by Fred Gaffen. Although some units included significant numbers of Indians (during World War I, the 114th — the Haldimand Rifles — recruited extensively among the Six Nations) neither the Department of Militia and Defence (DMD) during World War I, nor the Department of National Defence (DND) during World War II, officially kept their record of Indians distinct from non-Indians. It is fortunate for those tracing the service career of an Indian that the DIA did. For World War I service there is an especially useful nominal index of Indian soldiers that provides their unit name as well as reference to DIA case files in RG 10, vol. 11190. During the 1914–18 war, Indian agents were directed to provide headquarters with regular lists of enlistments, records that are now found in the Red Series of central registry headquarters files.[64] These reports usually provide, at minimum, the name, rank, unit and civil status of the soldier. Other records in these files may include more detail concerning an enlistee, such as number of children, religion, age and remarks concerning service. Some photographs are also found on file, as are letters by, or about, individual Indian soldiers.

Pay Allowances, Pensions, Those Killed or Wounded

The Red Series files also include the general correspondence concerning the arrangements for payment of separation allowances to the dependants of Indians on active service, and the payment of pensions to Indian veterans or to the surviving dependants of those killed. There is further general correspondence in the Headquarters central registry files series concerning World War I enlistments, including lists of Indians killed, wounded and discharged. It is here, as well, that the extensive block of case files relating to separation allowances, assigned pay, pensions and estates of deceased Indian soldiers is found.[65]

Records relating to World War II service are also found in the above-noted Headquarters central registry system series although there are considerably fewer case files relating to this war. There are general files concerning enlistment and discharges, deserters, and lists of Indians wounded and killed. There is also correspondence concerning national registration. There is a small, but rich, series relating to the Indians of British Columbia in World War II in the records of the Office of the Indian Commissioner for British Columbia (ICBC), and another in the Campbell River District Office, records originally from the Kwawkewlth Agency. Included are general files relating to enlistments and national registration as well as dependants' allowances, Veterans' Land Act (VLA) grants, training, deferments and refusals to report. There is also a series of individual agency enlistment files.[66]

Veterans of Both World Wars

The special arrangements made during and after both wars to provide land for returned soldiers are also documented in RG 10. Under the Soldier Settlement Act (SSA)[67] of 1919, the Soldier Settlement Board was given powers to provide assistance to veterans. Because of the unique relationship between Indians and the Crown, the DIA was given the responsibility to administer the provisions of the Act on behalf of Indians. Loans were made available to individual returned Indian soldiers for the purchase of land, stock and equipment. Accounting record of these loans is available in a Soldier Settlement Fund ledger that includes individual entries for each loan holder, arranged by agency, detailing loan amounts, items purchased and repayment schedules.[68] Ledger entries also provide references to the related files that are found in the Headquarters central registry system series.

Included in those records are both general files and individual soldier case files. The latter contain correspondence and other records of loan applications, the purchases made with loan monies, repayments and DIA inspectors' reports on loan holders. All but four of the case files are fully open to research; they are referenced in the finding aid by name of soldier.[69]

Provision was likewise made for veterans of service in World War II. The Veterans' Land Act (VLA), 1942,[70] provided that grants could be made to eligible Indian veterans to settle on Indian reserve lands and Section 35A of the act set out the purposes for which grants could be made, the said grants to be approved by the Director, VLA, and to be controlled and managed in trust on behalf of the Indian veteran by the Minister responsible for Indian Affairs.

VLA Grants for Indian Veterans

While there are a number of agency case files relating specifically to Indian veterans from Nova Scotia, New Brunswick and Prince Edward Island in the Maritime field office records,[71] the largest block of RG 10 records relating to the administration of VLA grants for Indians is in the microform case files in the Headquarters central registry system series. The typical file contains the DIA's "Veterans' Land Act Application and Requisition for Grant" form that identifies and describes the applicant (name, band, ticket number, regimental number and rank, address, enlistment and discharge dates, age, marital status, whether or not pensioner, number of children, their age and sex, health, any previous VLA benefits) and indicates the amount of grant requested and purpose to which the money was to be put. This form is usually accompanied by a copy of DND's service record for the individual (which includes date and place of birth, date of enlistment and discharge, overseas service, medals, rank, reason for discharge and physical description), or a DVA "Record of Service in the Canadian Army" form, or a copy of a discharge certificate.

Other standard documents in the files include the DVA's "Soldier Settlement and Veterans Land Act" form detailing the veteran's Re-establishment Credit (that is, the dollar amount of VLA benefit to which he was entitled) and the DIA's VLA form certifying to the delivery of the goods/chattels purchased (a document made out by the vendor of the goods to prove he had delivered the goods asked for in the veteran's application). Some files also include copies of Band Council Resolutions, correspondence regarding the benefit and the DIA's "VLA Report" form (a document signed by the Indian Superintendent and recording purchases made by the veteran).

Chapter Four

RG 10 Sources for Non-Status Aboriginal People

RG 10 is most valuable as a genealogical source for status Indians. They are, after all, the reason for which the DIA exists. Record Group 10 is, at best, a limited source for information relating to those individual Aboriginal people who do not fit the definition of "Indian" as set out in the Indian Act. This is simply explained by the fact that, by definition, those people are not the administrative responsibility of the DIA.

The Inuit

In the case of the Inuit, there are other records in Library and Archives Canada custody that are extremely important and useful, particularly those in RG 85 — the records of the Northern Affairs administration in the present-day Department of Indian Affairs and Northern Development (DIAND).[72] It is there that a considerable amount of individual-level information on Inuit people is found. By virtue of the geographical location and nomadic lifestyle of the Inuit, the long arm of the federal government reached them relatively late. As with Indians, so for the Inuit: there are important non-government records such as private manuscripts of explorers, traders and missionaries that will offer some individual-level information.[73]

The Métis and Non-status Indians

Ironically the Métis and non-status Indian populations are documented in the RG 10 record to the extent that they are, more than anything else by virtue of the DIA's need to record their exclusion from departmental responsibility. As noted already, the notion of "status Indian," and the enshrining in law of distinctions between elements of the Aboriginal population, came about only in the latter half of the nineteenth century. The disturbances surrounding the entry of Manitoba into Confederation had the effect of forcing the federal government to deal with the land claims of the Métis and, in so doing, to construct two separate methods of compensating for the extinguishment of Aboriginal title: treaty for Indians; scrip in the form of land or money for the "half-breeds". [Here I use the terminology that, although it came to take on a pejorative connotation in more recent times, was in widespread use in the late-nineteenth century and is invariably used in the documents.]

The settlement of "half-breed" claims, and the distribution of compensation in lands or money, was the responsibility of the Department of the Interior and not the DIA. The primary government records that document this process are found today at the LAC in the historical records found in RG 15 — Department of the Interior. What is found in RG 10 relates primarily to those people whose status might be termed to have been ambiguous, who did not fall clearly into one or the other category or who managed to move from one category to the other over time.

The 1876 Indian Act was the first to include in its definition of Indian status a specific exclusion of those who had benefitted from the settlement with the Métis. Section 3(3)(e) provided that

> no half-breed in Manitoba who has shared in the distribution of half-breed lands shall be accounted an Indian; and that no half-breed head of family (except the widow of an Indian, or a half-breed who has already been admitted into a treaty), shall, unless under very special circumstances, to be determined by the Superintendent General or his agent, be accounted an Indian, or entitled to be admitted into any Indian treaty.[74]

An amendment to this section three years later provided further that any "half-breed" who had been admitted to treaty would be allowed to withdraw therefrom with certain penalties.

Expansion into the West

In these early years of federal expansion into the West there was a certain fluidity in the movement of the Aboriginal population, with people being enrolled in treaty and then with-drawing in order to avail themselves of the more immediately tangible benefit of "half-breed" scrip, some only to be re-admitted to treaty in spite of the legislation. The interpretation of DIA policy obviously caused some problems for officers in the field as is evidenced by the records that survive. There are a number of files in the Black Series headquarters central registry files that document these movements. A cursory search of the automated finding aid to the Black Series using the keyword "half-breed" reveals some 160 file references. Included are files relating to individual cases of scrip-taking and its impact on treaty rights and status of the people involved; case files concerning the re-entry into treaty of individuals who had taken scrip; a number of files dealing with groups of people who took or applied to take scrip; and a number of more general files of a policy nature.[75]

RG 10 also includes a small number of registers relating to those people who applied to withdraw from treaty to take scrip, those who actually withdrew and received scrip and those who subsequently re-entered treaty. Included are a nominal index of applications to leave treaty and take scrip, 1870–1920 (RG 10, vol. 10035); a register of names of "half-breeds" withdrawn from treaty, 1885–1886 in the Manitoba Superintendency (RG 10, vol. 10037); a list of "half-breeds" who had withdrawn from treaty, 1 June 1888 (RG 10, vol.10038); a statement of half-breeds who had received scrip and re-entered treaty, Treaty 5, Pas and Cumberland bands (RG 10, vol. 10039); and a register of "half-breeds" who applied to withdraw from treaty, 1886–1926 (RG 10, vol. 10040).[76]

Treaty Annuity Lists

Because they record withdrawals and discharges from treaty, as well as active membership, the treaty annuity paylists, while primarily a record of payments made to those entitled to share in the benefits of treaty, are also of some interest to those tracing non-status Indian Aboriginal ancestors. Because they are, as described in an earlier discussion, for the period prior to 1951, an important record of status and band membership, they are equally a record of those whose status was challenged and changed. They are especially useful in identifying those Indian women who lost their status through marriage to non-Indians since, as mentioned earlier, loss of status did not, until the changes brought about by the 1951 Indian Act, necessarily mean removal from the paylists. These women came to be known as "red ticket women" from the colour of the special card issued to show their continued treaty status even though they had lost their Indian status.

Individual band membership and commutation files and, in certain instances, those files relating to the payment of treaty annuities, can also be important sources for tracing non-status Indians, both those whose status was never recognized and those who lost it. The appearance of a person claiming eligibility to enter treaty or removal from eligibility was virtually always reason for correspondence to headquarters with details of the case.

Application of Henrietta McRae, St.Peter's Band, Manitoba, to withdraw from Treaty under the terms of section 14 of the Indian Act of 1880, dated 15 December 1885/Library and Archives Canada/C-142518

Superannuated
Mar. 31, 1912   Joseph deLisle

Contributed to Superan Fund.   file 7066
                                                148749 (Clerk)

Rank or Class 3d Class

Date of appointment 23d June 1880

Salary on appointment, $ 600

Reported for duty

To fill a vacancy or new appointment New appointment

Province to which he belonged at time of appointment Quebec

Appointment confirmed by Order in Council of

Passed Civil Service Preliminary Examination on the   18   , at

Passed Civil Service Qualifying Examination on the   18   , at

Date, year and place of birth 15th Feby 1860   Caughnawaga, P.Q.

Origin and Religion Indian   Roman Catholic

Oaths of allegiance and office taken and subscribed 29th Nov. 1888 and 25th Jan. 1901

REMARKS Employed as an Extra Clerk from 8th July 1879
until appointment.
Granted leave for one month from 22 June 1898 on a/c inflammation of
the eyes; two months from 18 June 1900; from 13 May to 9 Oct. 1903.
Passed promotion exam" for Second Class in May 1894. Granted leave from
Aug. 1 to Nov. 1, 1909, owing to illness; to Feb 1, 1910; to May 1, 1910; to Aug. 1, 1910.

YEARLY SALARY.

Day	Month	Year	Salary	Rank or Class	Day	Month	Year	Salary	Rank or Class	Day	Month	Year	Salary	Rank or Class
23	June	1880	600	3d	1	July	1899	1000						
1	July	1881	650	"	1	Jan.	1900	1000	Jr 2					
1	July	1883	700	"	1	Jan.	1904	1050	"					
1	July	1884	750	"	1	Jan.	1905	1100	"					
1	July	1885	800	"	1	Feb.	1905	1200	S. 2					
1	July	1886	850	"	1	Apr.	1906	1250	"					
1	July	1887	900	"	1	Apr.	1907	1300	"					
1	July	1888	950	"	1	Apr.	1908	1350	"					
					1	Sept.	1908	1500	2-B					
					1	April	1909	1550	"					
					1	April	1910	1600	"					

PROMOTION, OR OTHER CHANGE OF POSITION IN DEPARTMENT.

Promoted to 2nd Class Feb. 1, 1905, vice Mr. H. J. Brook, superannuated, by O.C. of Dec. 31, 1904.
Promotion confirmed Mar. 6, 1906. Classified as Clerk in Subdivision B of Second
Division, $1350, under C.S. Amendment Act, 1908. Sal. incr. to $1500 by Act. No 187
of Statutes of 1909. Superannuated from Mar. 31, 1912, allowance $1013.33.

Entry from DIA Establishment Book for Joseph de Lisle, clerk in the Inside Service from 1880 to 1912, one of the few Indian employees at that time/Library and Archives Canada/C-142520

Chapter Five

The Records: RG 10 Sources for DIA Employees

The third group of individuals on whom RG 10 holdings shed light is that which I have termed "DIA employees." For purposes of this discussion, I have included in this category not only those who were officially designated as employees (under whichever of the changing public service regulations was in force at the time) but also those whose activities were subsidized by the DIA, such as teachers in denominational schools or doctors to whom DIA paid a retainer for services. Even with this expanded definition, the point to bear in mind is that this group is relatively small. Nevertheless, for those with an ancestor who falls within this category, or those biographers of DIA officials, there is material of value.

There are two broad types of employee-related records: those that were created to document the service of an individual — what might be termed "personnel" records — and those operational records, of whatever subject matter, that were created by, or about, an identifiable individual in the course of his or her duties that can give the researcher some insight into that person's life through his or her daily work (for example, the official reports of an Indian agent that include personal observations on an event). There are a number of miscellaneous indexes, most of which were prepared in the DIA by its staff to assist in keeping track of staff both present and past, and that now form part of RG 10. See, for example, the "Who Was Who and When" (RG 10, vols. 737 and 11189), the "Historical Directory of Indian Agents and Agencies" (RG 10, vol. 11190), indices to appointments and service of individuals who were not DIA officers (RG 10, vol. 11189) and long-serving departmental Secretary J. D. McLean's "Biographies and Scrapbook" (RG 10, vol. 11189). Among the scattered miscellaneous records relating to individual employees are the individual accounts in the Trust Fund ledgers. These records are, for the most part, accounts of monies held in trust by the government for the benefit of individual Indians or bands. However, the ledgers include approximately 125 accounts opened in the names of DIA employees. Most pre-date 1900 and are only in existence for a few years. They are identified by name of account holder in the appropriate RG 10 finding aid.

Personnel Records

Civil Service Lists and the DIA's Annual Reports

Anyone who has traced the career of an ancestor who served with the federal government will be well aware of the published Civil Service List[77] in which you will find such information as title of position held and, sometimes, branch of department; dates of first and present appointment; salary; and date of birth. In the case of the DIA, the published *Annual Report*[78] for the period up to World War I also includes tables listing the staff of both the "Inside" and the "Outside" services. In addition there are the personnel files of certain public servants that have been retained for historical purposes at LAC in RG 32 (the Historical Personnel Files collection). There are also historical personnel records in RG 10. Because, until relatively recently, the Aboriginal component of DIA staff was quite small, these records relate largely to non-Indians, although there are examples of Aboriginal staff dating to the late-ninteenth century.

The Establishment Books

The series known as the Establishment Books[79] is particularly useful. These ledgers, maintained to keep track of staff and their salaries, took slightly different forms over the years from about 1860 to 1955. Some record only the "Inside" service, others only the "Outside" service, and still others, both.[80] Some are arranged by date of appointment, and not always with a nominal index. Others are organized alphabetically by name of individual in groupings by province and territory. The illustration on page 42 is an example.

The earliest Establishment Books, those dating from the latter half of the nineteenth century, record the name, position held, date and place of birth, nationality, religion, date of first appointment to the public service, salary and "general observations" (including, where applicable, previous positions held and salaries, promotions, dates of resignation/dismissal or death). Reference to a personnel file is also usually provided. Later versions of this record include largely the same information but with even greater detail of career and salary progression. Some books include such information as educational level attained and military service.

As the range of services provided by the DIA expanded in the twentieth century, of course, a wider range of personnel came to be included in this record (for example, nurses at Indian hospitals, medical dispensers, Indian constables and doctors are included among the clerks, stenographers, Indian agents, farm instructors and other staff). Teachers, who were still nominated by the various religious denominations by the time these records end, were not considered salaried employees and, therefore, are not included.

Finding Aids to Personnel Records

Personnel files can be found in RG 10 principally in the two sub-series of the Headquarters central registry system series for the period c.1870–1923 — the Red and Black series. In the RG 10 finding aids to these records, such files will be found indexed by employee name. Most of these records, it would seem, were originally created to document appointments, with records of other aspects of an employee's career then added. These files exist not only for the senior members of the service but also for the very junior — the typists, stenographers and junior clerks. The circumstances of appointments are documented as are resignations or dismissals. As the variables of each case warrant, there might be record of leave taken or of pensions paid to an employee or surviving spouse. There may also be comments relating to the employee's work (both good and bad) with references to disciplinary actions or particular recommendations of praise.

Names Are Not Necessarily Indexed

Both the Red and Black series also include a number of more general files concerning staff, such as lists and returns of agents, physicians, teachers or even missionaries, with various information recorded. Individual names do not appear in the file titles of any of these files, nor are the records found together in blocks. Each file tends to be a return of information for a limited time period only. Sample files include lists of agents, missionaries, physicians and teachers employed by the DIA, 1880–1881; list of names, nationality, religion and salary of staff, 1882; correspondence regarding missionaries who engaged in trade with the Indians, 1887–1909; list of DIA employees, including a complete list of medical officers, 1922–1934.[81] In addition, there are records that describe the work performed in different areas of the department, records that can help explain exactly what it meant for your ancestor to spend his or her working life as a clerk in a turn-of-the-century government office or as an Indian agent on the Prairies.[82]

Teachers in the Church Schools

Teachers in Indian schools are more difficult to document within RG 10 primarily because, during the period of denominational running of the schools, they were employees not of the DIA but of the various churches. School inspection reports do exist, some from the late-nineteenth century,[83] but while these can be quite good for information about curriculum and conditions, there is relatively little comment about the teacher. For the period c.1870–1965, there are a large number of "general administration" files relating to education and to individual schools in the Headquarters central registry system series. These files reveal much about policy and day-to-day administration of Indian education and do contain information about individual teachers (including in some cases their applications to teach, which provide personal and educational qualification information), their salaries and living and working conditions. Such records are organized by agency, of course, and will be located through the finding aids to these series by name of agency or school name.

There are also "school establishment" files for the post–World War I period in the Headquarters central registry system records (RG 10, vols. 8596–8615) that include general records relating to methods of appointment and teacher salary schedules, and such specific records as teacher applications. There are also files for individual schools' staff that include correspondence relating to the hiring of individual teachers, their salaries and completed application forms. A small block of teacher application files from the 1940s and 1950s is also found in the School Files series.[84]

Records Documenting Public Careers in the DIA

Biographical Information

Within RG 10, as indeed would be the case within any records of federal government agencies, there is a certain amount of biographical information that one can draw from a reading of the records that document an individual's work activities. No biography of such historical figures as Sir William Johnson, Sir John Johnson, Duncan Campbell Scott, Clifford Sifton or even Sir John A. Macdonald would be complete without reference to their public careers in Indian Affairs. For such biographical studies the public record is an important complement to private manuscript collections.

Duncan Campbell Scott is a case in point. A biographer searching the private papers in the custody of the LAC would scarcely realize that this man, prominent in Canadian literary and cultural circles for over a quarter century, was a career public servant and, indeed, occupied the highest position within the DIA for over two decades.[85]

Obviously those individuals just cited were prominent figures who had significant careers both inside and outside the DIA. Yet, for anyone whose ancestor served with the DIA or, as was the case with missionaries, was likely either to have been reported upon by the DIA or interceded with the department on behalf of their charges, there is potential for information that will be of interest to your family. It is true that the formal reports of a civil servant to his superiors tend to be written in a manner in which the bureaucracy demands and, therefore, mask the personal feelings of the author. Nevertheless, those same records, even if they tell you little about the character of the individual, can be very revealing about the conditions in which he or she laboured.

Affidavit of Performance of Settlement Duties by William Clark, dated 13 June 1889, for Lot 27, Concession 7, Robinson Township, Manitoulin District, Ontario. The document attests to 20 acres cleared and under crop and a habitable house of 18' x 24'./Library and Archives Canada/C-142516

Chapter Six

Non-Native Dealings with the DIA and/or Status Indians

Of the four groups identified at the outset of this study, this is possibly the most difficult to document in RG 10 records because, for this group, the DIA record is a secondary source rather than a principal source of information. In the case of the status Indian population, the mandate of the DIA dictated that its activities would be documented at an individual level. The organizational demands of the bureaucracy ensured that the records relating to individuals employed by the department would be maintained. Records relating to non-Natives who had dealings with the DIA and its Indian charges, on the other hand, were created, not as a result of a primary function of the relationship between the department and the client, but as a result of an intercession of the department between its primary client — the Native Indian — and the wider society.

Aboriginal Land Dealings

The most obvious point of contact between the Aboriginal population and the broader Canadian society involved the exploitation of those resources belonging to the Indian, in particular land. The most fundamental principle of British, and then Canadian, Indian policy was that the Crown alone could deal in this commodity. The Royal Proclamation of 1763 explicitly forbade private purchases of Indian land, setting up the Crown, instead, as the intermediary in such transactions. European settlement would not be prohibited but, rather, the most rapacious aspects of its character regulated by ensuring that Indians could dispose of their lands only to the Crown.[86]

With a policy that Indian lands could be surrendered only to the Crown, with the benefit of their subsequent disposal to accrue to the Indians, it was incumbent upon the authorities to keep a record of the sales. That this was not always carefully done in the pre-Confederation period is clear.[87] Even where they were kept with reasonable care, pre-Confederation (or, more precisely, pre-file era) records relating to the disposal of Indian land are not straightforward in their use and can pose many problems for the researcher looking for information about an individual purchaser.

The earliest RG 10 series of incoming correspondence to the offices of the Governor General, the Lieutenant Governors, the Superintendent General, the Deputy Superintendent General of Indian Affairs (DSGIA) and the Chief Superintendent have no contemporary nominal or subject indexes. Their arrangement is chronological. One notable exception is the series of petitions to the Governor General for which there are contemporary abstract indexes.[88] Where letterbooks of outgoing replies to correspondence exist, they are normally indexed internally. However, such letterbooks do not exist for all series.

A portion of the incoming correspondence of the office of the Chief Superintendent in Upper Canada, c.1830–45, has an alphabetical/chronological arrangement that segregates letters according to correspondents whose names begin with the same letter of the alphabet. However, it is not really until the period beginning about 1845, when the office of the Civil Secretary takes on the role of central registration and control of the Indian Affairs correspondence, that proper indexing of the main correspondence of the DIA begins.

The same holds largely true for the records of the field offices in RG 10 for the pre-Confederation period. The surviving record falls broadly into one of three categories: incoming correspondence (usually arranged chronologically and, possibly, accompanied by contemporary subject/nominal indexes); letterbooks of outgoing replies (by their nature arranged chronologically and usually indexed); and miscellaneous records arranged in a variety of ways and rarely indexed nominally.

Land Matters in the Correspondence Files

Land matters will be found scattered throughout the main incoming correspondence and letterbook replies. Some of the miscellaneous records also specifically concern Indian lands. The Grand River claims records are an example. The validity of leases to Six Nations land was an issue of considerable dispute in early nineteenth century Upper Canada. The Commission of Trustees, appointed in 1834, heard over 200 claims arising from these leases and the records of these claims include schedules of names of landholders, petitions, sketch maps, correspondence and copies of indentures.[89]

Another example of a miscellaneous land record from the pre-Confederation period, that documents individual settlers' purchases, is the inspection return. For example, abstracts of returns of inspection exist for various Indian land sales in Upper Canada/Canada West for the years 1832–1865. These provide such information as lot and concession, number of acres and extent cleared, name of purchaser and occupant, sale date and number, and value of land improved and unimproved.[90] The illustration on page 50 is an example of an Upper Canada Inspection Return.

There are other miscellaneous pre-Confederation Indian land records scattered throughout RG 10. Included are records of the Montreal Superintendency (including such documents as the Caughnawaga and St. Regis leases, and land sales of Abenaki land in Durham Township); the Central Superintendency (including land sales and land returns for Tyendinaga, Mississaugas of the Credit, other central Ontario bands and Saugeen, including an extensive record from the Wiarton land office beginning in the late-eighteenth century and continuing into the twentieth); the Western Superintendency and the Northern Superintendency (the latter including both pre- and post-Confederation records).

The centralization of responsibility for Indian Affairs, after the transfer from Imperial to colonial control and the codification in subsequent federal Indian Acts and regulations of the procedures by which Indian lands would be disposed, helped ensure that a more thorough record of land transactions would be maintained in the post-Confederation period.

Start with the Indian Land Registry

Included among the major changes effected in the Indian Act in 1951 was the provision that the Department maintain a register of the particulars relating to the disposition of surrendered Indian lands. Although the Indian Land Registry was established only relatively recently, its staff made a concerted effort to review historical records when the registry was set up. They gathered as many original deeds and related land documents from the files as could be found. This effort involved the culling of records already in LAC custody and the removal of original documents from the files and their replacement in LAC files by copies. The Indian Land Registry today, then, serves a function for Indian lands similar to that performed by a provincial land registry office for non-Indian lands. That office is a logical starting point for any question about Indian land.

The Indian Land Registry still has in its custody land sales books covering transactions dating back into the nineteenth century. It is also the best source for information about patents to sold Indian lands. In 1886, the responsibility for issuing Indian land patents was transferred to the DIA from what was then the Registrar's Branch in the office of the Secretary of State. This responsibility was transferred back to the office of the Registrar General in 1930, and remains there today. Patent copies for the years 1886–1930 are part of the RG 10 holdings but their physical condition is such that, until conservation work is completed, they can be consulted only in special circumstances. Researchers requesting access to these records from RG 10 are directed to the Indian Land Registry in DIAND where microform copies are available for consultation and which are indexed by name of patentee and legal description.

Land Transactions in the East and the West

Within the Red and Black series of Headquarters central registry records there are hundreds of files relating to the individual purchases of, and the issuing of patents for, surrendered Indian land. These files are referenced in the finding aids to both series by name of patentee or purchaser. Most relate to transactions that took place in the late-nineteenth century.

The tremendous pressures placed upon Indian bands in the West — from the last decade of the nineteenth century — to surrender parts of their reserves so that the land could be opened to settlers and, after World War I, to returned soldiers, resulted in many large land sales on the Prairies. Indeed, so great was the sale activity that the DIA created a separate file classification system to deal with the records. The relevant files are now in RG 10, concentrated largely in the Headquarters central registry system series.[91]

This block of records contains general correspondence about each reserve land sale with information concerning the process by which the land was valued, the arrangements made for the sale (some were by tender, some by public auction) and the agent's report of the sale. These general files are accompanied by individual sale case files for each purchase. It is in these files that you can follow the history of each transaction from the original purchaser (frequently a land speculator who acquired large blocks) through the assignees to the point at which a patent was issued. Some case files contain little more than copies of departmental letters notifying purchasers of instalment payments due and of receipts for monies paid, or letters threatening re-possession for non-payment. Others, particularly those from Depression years, include the poignant letters of settlers struggling to keep their land. These case files are not consistently indexed in the finding aids by name of purchaser or assignee with the result that — in the majority of cases — anyone searching for an individual file needs to know the name of the band or reserve from which the land was originally surrendered.

Very few large surrenders for sale were taken after the 1920s. Rather, the emphasis shifted to the leasing of reserve land. There is a block of lease records, both general agency and individual case files.[92] Again, however, the researcher is wise to check for lease information through the Indian Land Registry.

As regards field office records relating to land sales or leases to individuals in the post-Confederation period, there are scattered records.[93] Some of the series for pre-Confederation land transactions, mentioned earlier, continue into the twentieth century (for example, the Wiarton land office records). There are other pockets of records such as leases and licences for timber. See the Timber Records series

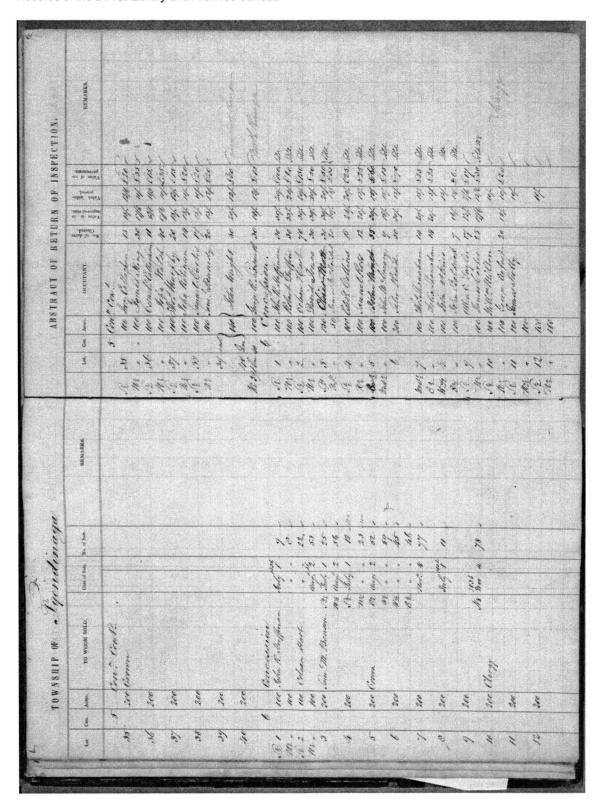

Township of Tyendinaga — Abstract of Inspection, 1836 showing Lot, Concession, acreage, to whom sold, occupant, acreage cleared, valuation/Library and Archives Canada/C-142514

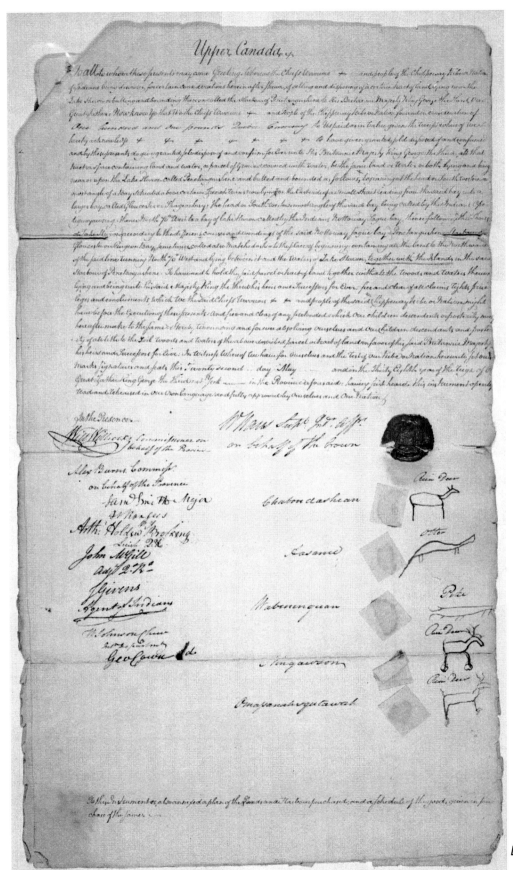

Surrender by the Chippeway [sic] Nation of lands and waters at the Harbour of Penetanguishene, 22 May 1798/ Library and Archives Canada/C-15390

in RG 10, some of the records of which relate to band member exploitation of reserve timber and some to non-Indian licences. However, because the function of recording land transactions came to be very centralized in DIA headquarters in the years following Confederation, the researcher is advised to exhaust all possibilities among the headquarters records before turning to field office sources.

Conclusion

The historical records of the Department of Indian Affairs in the custody of the Library and Archives Canada are, beyond doubt, an important source for individual-level information about status Indians. They are also, albeit to a lesser extent, a useful source for those whose research involves Aboriginal peoples other than status Indians, employees of the DIA and those members of the non-Aboriginal population who had dealings with status Indians or with the DIA. The nature of the historical relationship between the client department and its clientele has made this so. In many ways, the DIA has — historically at least — acted as a "government within a government" in performing, on behalf of the Indian people, tasks that would have been carried out for the non-Indian population by a range of government agencies at the federal, provincial and even municipal levels.

Centralization of responsibilities, and the concomitant centralization of the records documenting the performance of those responsibilities, presents both advantages and disadvantages to the researcher. "One-stop shopping" may appear to save time. Yet, in the pursuit of information — as in the search for any commodity — it is the wise consumer who compares a number of sources before deciding which are the most suitable. In certain spheres, and for certain time periods, the records of the DIA are virtually the single source of written evidence of the endeavours of the status Indian population in Canada. Moreover, even where other sources of information for an event exist (for example, in the records of missionaries, agents of other government departments or those of private individuals or corporations such as the Hudson's Bay Company) they tend also to present the evidence of observers from outside the Indian community. Until relatively recently, there are few accounts written by Indians of transactions in which they figured prominently.

RG 10 is not a consistently good source for all periods of time or for all of the varied First Nations throughout this geographically diverse country. It is most useful for those whose research focuses on the post-Confederation era. It includes virtually no record relating to the Indian population of Atlantic Canada before 1867, or of the Prairies or the North prior to the signing of the Western treaties. As well, unfortunately, it is too often the case that, even where different levels of the DIA bureaucracy each created a record of an event, only the headquarters documents have survived.

Yet, for all its imperfections, RG 10 continues to be heavily used by the Aboriginal research community. A not insignificant portion of that research is of a genealogical nature. While it might be said that the current interest in Native genealogical research is very much the product of the 1985 changes to the Indian Act, it is difficult to believe that the genie will return to the bottle once all the claims to status, based on those legislated amendments, have been researched and resolved. Genealogy is about heritage, not politics. Indeed, many Native communities already recognize the enormous cultural value to be derived from reconstructing their past with the aid of genealogical research. The measure of the success of guides such as this one will be the degree to which they assist in that endeavour.

Appendix A

Basic Steps in Researching Your Aboriginal Ancestry

* When researching your Aboriginal genealogy, you are actually asking one of the following questions:

The General Question

"My family has a tradition that we have an Aboriginal ancestor. How do I find out if this is true?"

The Legal Question

"I believe I am entitled to status under the Indian Act (or to legal membership in a particular First Nations community) because I am directly related to a Native person who did have status. How do I prove this?"

To answer either question, you must discover and carefully document your Aboriginal ancestry. This requires you to complete *two* interrelated steps:

STEP 1 Construct your family tree. Do the genealogical research and collect the family records needed to draw up your pedigree.

At the same time, your family research should be focused on trying to…

STEP 2 Identify your aboriginal ancestor. Identify, by name, exactly who in your family background was (or might have been) an Aboriginal person. The evidence collected must document a direct relationship between that person and yourself.

If you are also seeking to prove your legal status, you must go on to:

STEP 3 Contact the local regional office of the Department of Indian and Northern Affairs Canada. A listing of their offices is available in the telephone book's blue pages, toll-free at 1-800-567-9604, or on-line at **www.ainc-inac.gc.ca**. Be sure to explain your situation, obtain the forms needed to submit your evidence, and confirm that the documents you plan to submit are suitable for them to act upon. Many bands have opted to maintain their own registration lists.

STEP 4 Organize the legal proof of your ancestor's Native status. Gather legal (e.g., certified or notarized) copies of the documents that prove that this Aboriginal person was legally recognized as having First Nations status (and band membership, if appropriate). You will be using both regular genealogical records and special Indian membership sources.

STEP 5 Submit your claim to Indian and Northern Affairs Canada for a decision and approval.

* Permission to use this document is on page ii.

Steps 1 and 2   Constructing Your Family Pedigree

If you have no experience in doing family history, reading several how-to books on basic genealogical research methodology, available at any public library, will save you endless trouble. Several of the better-known authors and titles are listed in the Bibliography. You can also join the local genealogical society or genealogy club to take advantage of its members' expertise and of any courses or seminars that are offered. See Appendix C for further details.

When doing your family history, remember:

- Research and draw up a regular family pedigree. Focus on your direct relationship to the parent, grandparent, or great-grandparent who may have had Aboriginal ancestry.

- You must document your ancestry to a specific individual. Linking yourself to a community, ethnic group, or First Nations reserve is not enough.

- Begin with yourself and your immediate family, then work backwards by documenting each generation. Don't rush to the archival record expecting to find your surname or your suspected Native ancestor. Take the time to discover how past societies interacted and what records they created. Each of the First Nations are unique and the resources and records they have made available may vary dramatically. Learn how to ask the right questions.

- Record the source and reference code of every document you collect! This is critical to proving your Native ancestry, as any documents without citations will be rejected! If you are unsure how to fully cite your documents, ask the archives or library staff you are dealing with for advice.

- Use the records of that time and place that are most likely to name Aboriginal people. These will include the Department of Indian Affairs records discussed in this book, mission registers, Hudson's Bay Company and fur trade employee lists, and the trading post and survey records found in provincial or religious archives.

- Identify the person in your family tree who was most likely to have had Aboriginal status. Try to confirm his or her name(s), and the specific community or region where they lived, and the years when they were there. This is vital to finding other supporting records.

- Except for recent Band and Treaty Lists, very few records are arranged or indexed by surname. Most records were created or compiled on a year-by-year basis, or by subject. As a result, research in both restricted and open records is very time consuming.

- The use of European (English, French, or Spanish) surnames, even in earliest records, is no proof that the person had any European ancestry. Many Aboriginal people adopted non-Native names for personal or religious reasons.

- The spelling of Aboriginal names can vary wildly in the records, even when written by people who spoke the Native language, and especially by visiting officials who could not. Try to confirm which language your ancestors spoke. People who still use that vernacular may help you understand the meanings of the names you find. Be warned that there are, or has been, over 200 Aboriginal languages spoken in Canada. Dialects called "Indian", like "Indian Princesses", never existed.

Institutions Holding Aboriginal Genealogical Information

- Elders and members of Aboriginal community councils. For a listing of Aboriginal organizations, Tribal Councils, and First Nations, see *Akwesasne to Wunnumin Lake: profiles of Aboriginal communities in Ontario* (Toronto: Ontario Native Affairs Secretariat and Ministry of Citizenship, 1992). Check your library or the Internet for similar listings of Canada's First Nations communities (a few are listed in the Bibliography). Another good place to start is the web link page of the Ontario Native Affairs Secretariat at **www.nativeaffairs.jus.gov.on.ca**

- Library and Archives Canada Record Group 10, containing the early records of the Department of Indian Affairs, is not the only source for Aboriginal research in their holdings. Ask about other records that are available for the dates and locations you are interested in or consult their web pages on Aboriginal peoples at **www.collectionscanada.ca**

- The Provincial and Territorial Archives for the region in which you are researching. Many are placing their inventories on-line or have help sheets for those doing Aboriginal research. For a listing of these government archives, see Appendix B or check out **www.archivescanada.ca**

- The Provincial vital statistics offices for birth, marriage and death records. The vital statistics legislation for each province varies widely as to the date of creation, what information was collected, and what years are publicly accessible. Some early registrations have been transferred to the provincial archives, as in Ontario and British Columbia. Always ask for the most detailed format of the records and, if submitting them for status purposes, check if your records need to be certified.

- Church and mission archives may be the only source for school or vital statistics records for the region and the years in which your ancestor lived. A listing of the various church archival repositories is available in the *Canadian Almanac and Directory* or on-line from the Canadian Council of Archives (**www.cdncouncilarchives.ca**) and the University of Saskatchewan Archives' Canadian Archival Resources on the Internet listing (**www.usask.ca/archives/menu.html**).

As a rule, the Library and Archives of Canada and the various provincial and territorial archives will hold the older written sources while Indian And Northern Affairs Canada and the provincial vital statistics offices have the more recent records.

The provincial and territorial archives and the Library and Archives of Canada have been actively microfilming their governmental holdings and private collections for decades. Many of these micro-films are available on inter-library loan or have been purchased by local archives and libraries. As a result, much of your preliminary research could be done without having to travel to Ottawa or the region your Aboriginal ancestors lived. However, many Indian And Northern Affairs Canada records have not been copied and must be examined on site at Terrasses de la Chaudière, 10 Wellington, North Tower, Gatineau, Quebec.

Step 3   Discuss Status Claim with The Department of Indian Affairs Membership Office

Contact your local Indian Affairs office (a list is available from the telephone book's blue pages, on-line at **www.ainc-inac.gc.ca**, or from toll-free at 1-800-567-9604). Find out the latest developments in applying for status as important changes have been made to the Indian Act since June 1985 to bring it into line with the Canadian Charter of Rights and Freedoms. The Indian And Northern Affairs Canada Web site has extensive information on status and Treaty Rights, the various benefits and services available, and the necessary forms that can be downloaded. A comprehensive guide is the publication You Wanted to Know (R32-107, 1999) which is available from their Web site or upon request.

Be sure to obtain the correct application forms, as there are different requirements for those born before or after 17 April 1985, for disabled individuals, and for band membership. These forms can include:

- Request for Personal Information by Native Claims Researchers (10-513 E, Oct 2000)
- Application for Certificate of Indian Status (83-009 E, Jan 2001)
- Application for Registration of an Adult Under the Indian Act (83-044 E, Jan 2001)
- Application for Registration of a Child Under the Indian Act (83-044A E, Jan 2001)

Be sure to confirm what documentation will be accepted in support for your claim. Carefully follow any advice offered. Be aware that it may be hard to document Aboriginal ancestors more than three generations away from you (i.e., before the 1920s), and, therefore, very difficult to claim status from anyone before that time. Indian And Northern Affairs Canada will not search your status for you, or even advise you in detail on possible sources of information.

Also, since the passage of Bill C-31 in 1985, obtaining personal First Nations (Indian) status from Indian And Northern Affairs Canada, and being accorded First Nations band membership by a Native community, are two separate submissions. Becoming a Registered Indian does not make you a member of a First Nation. If the First Nation to which you ancestor belonged is one of the 250 First Nations that now controls its own membership, you must apply directly to them for membership. To learn more about reserve rights, Indian registration, the issuance of Certificates of Indian Status, Band lists, and the transfer of Band membership, contact the council for that First Nation or the Indian And Northern Affairs' Regional Director of Lands and Trust Services (Ottawa, Ontario KIA 0H4)

Step 4   Assemble Legal Proof of the Ancestor's Status

1. Get legal copies of all key official documents proving your direct linage back to an Aboriginal ancestor. For example, vital statistics, census, church and education records, etc. When duplicating historical records, request that they be legally certified as "true copies" by the institution supplying the copies.

2. Assemble the material by person and by year to conclusively document your step-by-step link to the individual supposedly having legal status.

3. Check with a legal advisor about "soft" or non-official documentation showing family connections, such as oral interviews with relatives, notarized statements and affidavits concerning a person's parentage or marriage, residency records, newspaper articles, wedding announcements, obituaries, cemetery headstones, military records etc.

If you have not already done so, you must now use the Library and Archives of Canada's Department of Indian Affairs (Record Group 10) records described in this book and those of Indian And Northern Affairs Canada to prove your ancestor's First Nations status. To find the membership records of the Department of Indian Affairs, write to the Ottawa offices of Indian And Northern Affairs Canada, 10 Wellington Street, Gatineau, Quebec K1A 0H4. These include:

- Treaty annuity paylists ("treaty paylists") for those areas where treaties were signed (from 1850 onwards, and for some areas of Canada only).
- Interest distribution paylists.

- Informal Indian membership lists for specific communities (before 1951).
- The Indian Register (from 1951 to the present).
- Enfranchisement records.
- First Nations band voters' lists.

For additional information on using the above records, see the section on "Indian status, membership and family history," on pages 130–149 of Bennett McCardle's two-volume *Indian History and Claims: A Research Handbook* (Ottawa: Indian And Northern Development, 1982).

Because some records contain personal information on living people, you may find that access to them is restricted by federal or provincial privacy legislation. This does not mean that these records are forever inaccessible but that the release of this information is done according to an established set of exemptions. Several First Nations councils have also restricted access to their band lists and membership registers. In both cases, you will need written permission from the council to see their records or will have to submit a formal request to the government office for information under their control.

Step 5   Submit Your Claim to Indian And Northern Affairs Canada for a Decision

It is hoped that these guidelines, the contents of this book and a large dose of patience, persistence and precision, will help locate your Aboriginal ancestors. Whether doing family history or researching your status or band membership…

Good luck!

Appendix B

Archives and Vital Statistics Offices

National Archives

Library and Archives Canada (LAC)
395 Wellington Street
Ottawa, ON K1A 0N4
Tel: 613-996-7458
Fax: 613-995-6274
www.collectionscanada.ca

Provincial Archives

Provincial Archives of Alberta
12845-102 Avenue North West
Edmonton, AB T5N 0M6
Tel: 780-427-1056
Fax: 780-427-4646
www.gov.ab.ca/mcd/mhs/paa/paa.htm

B.C. Archives
655 Belleville Street, Victoria
mailing address: Box 9419
Station Provincial Government
Victoria, BC V8V 9V1
Tel: 250-387-1952
Fax: 250-387-2072
www.bcarchives.gov.bc.ca

Provincial Archives of Manitoba
200 Vaughan Street
Winnipeg, MB R3C 1T5
Reference: 204-945-3971
Fax: 204-948-2008
www.gov.mb.ca/chc/archives/index.html

Provincial Archives of New Brunswick
Dineen Drive, UNB Campus Fredericton
mailing address: Box 6000
Fredericton, NB E3B 5H1
Tel: 506-453-2122
Fax: 506-453-3288
www.gov.nb.ca/supply/archives

Provincial Archives of Newfoundland and Labrador
Colonial Building, Military Road
St. John's, NL A1C 2C9
Tel: 709-729-3065
Fax: 709-729-0578
www.gov.nf.ca/panl/

Northwest Territories Archives
Prince of Wales Northern Heritage Centre
Box 1320
Yellowknife, NT X1A 2L9
Tel: 867-873-7657
Fax: 867-873-0205
www.pwnhc.learnnet.nt.ca/programs/archives.htm

Public Archives of Nova Scotia
6016 University Avenue
Halifax NS B3H 1W4
Tel: 902-424-6060
Fax: 902-424-0628
www.nsarm.ednet.ns.ca

Nunavut Archives
P.O. Box 310
Igloolik NV X0A 0L0
Tel: 867-934-8626
E-mail: eatkinson@gov.nv.ca

Public Archives of Nova Scotia
6016 University Avenue
Halifax, NS B3H 1W4
Tel: 902-424-6060
Fax: 902-424-0628
www.nsarm.ednet.ns.ca

Archives of Ontario
77 Grenville Street, Unit 300
Toronto, ON M5S 1B3
Tel: 416-327-1582
Fax: 416-327-1999
www.gov.on.ca/MCZCR/archives

Public Archives and Records Office of
Prince Edward Island
4th floor, Hon. George Coles Building,
Richmond Street, Charlottetown
mailing address: Box 1000
Charlottetown, PE C1A 7M4
Tel: 902-368-4290
Fax: 902-368-6327
www2.gov.pe.ca/educ/archives

Direction des Archives Nationales de l'Est du Québec
Pavillon Louis-Jacques Cassault
1210 avenue du Seminaire, Sainte-Foy
mailing address: C.P. 10450
Sainte-Foy, QC G1V 4N1
Tel: 418-643-8904
Fax: 418-646-0868
www.anq.gouv.qc.ca

Direction des Archives Nationales de l'Ouest du Québec
535, avenue Viger est
Montréal, QC H2L 2P3
Tel: 514-873-6000
Fax: 514-873-2950
www.anq.gouv.qc.ca
[Presumably, either of these central administrations will direct your query to the appropriate regional centre.]

Saskatchewan Archives Board
University of Saskatchewan, Rm 91
Murray Building
3 Campus Drive
Saskatoon, SK S7N 5A4
Tel: 306-933-5832
Fax: 306-933-7305
www.gov.sk.ca/govt/archives

Saskatchewan Archives Board
University of Regina
3737 Wascana Parkway
Regina, SK S4S 0A2
Tel: 306-787-4068
Fax: 306-787-1179
www.gov.sk.ca/govt/archives

Yukon Territory Archives
Box 2703, 400 College Drive
Whitehorse, YT Y1A 2C6
Tel: 867-667-5321
Fax: 867-393-6253
www.yukoncollege.yk.ca/archives/yukarch.html

Vital Statistics Offices

Alberta Government Services
Registries Division
Box 2023
Edmonton, AB T5J 4W7
Tel: 780-427-2683
Fax: 780-422-4225
www.gov.ab.ca/ma

British Columbia
Vital Statistics Agency
818 Fort Street, Victoria
mailing address: Box 9657
Station Provincial Government
Victoria, BC V8W 9P3
Tel: 250-952-2681
Fax: 250-952-2576
www.hlth.gov.bc.ca/vs/

Manitoba Consumer & Corporate Affairs, Vital Statistics
254 Portage Avenue
Winnipeg, MB R3C 0B6
Tel: 204-945-3701
Fax: 204-948-3128
www.gov.mb.ca

New Brunswick Department of Health &
Community Services
Vital Statistics
Box 6000
Fredericton, NB E3B 5H1
Tel: 506-453-7411
Fax: 506-453-3245
www.gov.nb.ca/hcs-ssc

Newfoundland and Labrador Department of
Government Services & Lands Vital Statistics Division
5 Mews Place, St. John's
mailing address: Box 8700
St. John's, NL A1B 4J6
Tel: 709-729-3311
Fax: 709-729-2071
www.gov.nf.ca/gsl/

Northwest Territories Dept. of Health & Social Services
Vital Statistics
Bag 9
Inuvik, NT X0E 0T0
Tel: 867-777-7420
Fax: 867-777-3197
www.gov.nt.ca/

Nova Scotia Department of Business &
Commercial Services
Vital Statistics
Joseph Howe Building
1690 Hollis Street, Halifax
mailing address: Box 157
Halifax, NS B3J 2M9
Tel: 902-424-4381
Fax: 902-424-0678
www.gov.ns.ca/bacs/vstat

Ontario Minister of Consumer & Commercial Relations
Registrar General Branch
189 Red River Road
Thunder Bay
mailing address, Box 4600
Thunder Bay, ON P7B 6L8
Tel: 1-800-461-2156
or: 416-325-8305
Fax: 807-343-7459
www.ccr.gov.on.ca/mccr

P.E.I. Department of Health and Social Services, Vital
Statistics
Box 3000
Montague, PE C0A 1R0
Tel: 902-838-0882
Fax: 902-838-0883
www.gov.pe.ca/hss/index.html
[use "search" or F A Questions]

Province du Québec
Le Directeur de L'Etat Civil
Service à la clientele
205 rue Montmagny
Québec, QC G1N 2Z9
Tel: (Québec) 418-643-3900; (Montréal) 514-864-3900
Elsewhere in Qué. 800-567-3900
Fax: 418-646-3255
www.etatcivil.gouv.qc.ca

Saskatchewan Health
Vital Statistics & Health
Insurance Registration Branch
1919 Rose Street
Regina, SK S4P 3V7
Tel: 306-787-1167
Fax: 306-787-8310
www.gov.sk.ca/govt/health

Yukon Health & Social Services
Vital Statistics
Box 2703
Whitehorse, YT Y1A 2C6
Tel: 867-667-5207
Fax: 867-393-3069
www.hss.gov.yk.ca/

Appendix C

Genealogical Societies

National

Canadian Federation of Genealogical & Family History Societies (CANFED)
227 Parkville Bay
Winnipeg, MB R2M 2J6
Tel: 204-256-6176

Société généalogique canadienne-française
3440, rue Davidson, Montréal
mailing address: C.P. 335, Station Place d'Armes
Montréal, QC H2Y 3H1
Tel: 514-527-1010
Fax: 514-527-0265
www.sgcf.com/

United Empire Loyalists' Association of Canada (UEL)
Suite 202, George Brown House
50 Baldwin Street
Toronto, ON M5T 1L4
Tel: 416-591-1783
Fax: 416-591-7506
www.npiec.on.ca/ uela/uela1.htm
The UEL Association has a number of branches across Canada that are not listed here; check the Web site.

Provincial

Alberta Genealogical Society (AGS)
Prince of Wales Armouries
Heritage Centre
#116 — 10440-108 Avenue
Edmonton, AB T5H 3Z9
Tel: 403-424-4429
Fax: 403-423-8980
www.compusmart.ab.ca/abgensoc
The Alberta Genealogical Society has branches throughout the province that are not listed here; check the Web site. The Alberta Family History Society is a separate organization in Calgary. It has no branches.

Alberta Family History Society (AFHS)
Box 30270, Station B
Calgary, AB T2M 4P1
Tel: 403-214-1447
www.afhs.ab.ca

British Columbia Genealogical Society (BCGS)
Box 88054, Lansdowne Mall
Richmond, BC V6X 3T6
Tel: (604-502-9119
Fax: 604-263-4952
www.npsnet.com/bcgs/
There are a individual local genealogical organizations throughout the province unaffiliated with the British Columbia Genealogical Society not listed here.

Victoria Genealogical Society (VGS)
Box 45031, Mayfair Postal Outlet
Victoria, BC V8Z 7G9
Tel: 250-360-2808
www.islandnet.com/ vgs/homepage.html

Manitoba Genealogical Society (MGS)
Unit A, 1045 St James Street
Winnipeg, MB R3H 1B1
Tel: 204-783-9139
Fax: 204-783-0190
www.mbnet.mb.ca/ mgs
The Manitoba Genealogical Society has branches throughout the province that are not listed here.

New Brunswick Genealogical Society (NBGS)
Box 3235, Station B
Fredericton, NB E3A 5G9
Telephone/Fax: [none noted]
www.bitheads.ca/nbgs/
The New Brunswick Genealogical Society is composed of representatives of each of its branches throughout the province that are not listed here. For further information, go to the NBGS Web site. As well, there are some independent groups in the province.

Centre d'études Acadiennes
Université de Moncton
Moncton, NB E1A 3E9
Tel: 506-858-4085
Fax: 506-858-4530
www.umoncton.ca/etudeacadiennes/centre/cea.html

Newfoundland & Labrador Genealogical Society, Inc. (NLGS)
Colonial Building, Military Road
St. John's, NL A1C 2C9
Tel: 709-754-9525
Fax: 709-754-6430
www3.nf.sympatico.ca/nlgs

Northwest Territories Genealogical Society (NTGS)
Box 1715
Yellowknife, NT X1A 2P3
Tel: [none noted]
Fax: 867-873-9304
www.ssimicro.com/nonprofit/nwtgs/

Genealogical Association of Nova Scotia (GANS)
Box 641, Station Central
Halifax, NS B3J 2T3
Tel: 902-454-0322
Fax: [none noted]
www.chebucto.ns.ca/Recreation/GANS/
Nova Scotia has a number of individual genealogical societies unaffiliated with The Genealogical Association of Nova Scotia that are not listed here.

Genealogical Institute of the Maritimes
P.O. Box 36022
Canada Post Postal Office
5675 Spring Garden Road
Halifax, NS B3J 1G0
nsgna.ednet.ns.ca

Ontario Genealogical Society (OGS)
102 — 40 Orchard View Blvd
Toronto, ON M4R 1B9
Tel: 416-489-0734
Fax: 416-489-9803
www.ogs.on.ca
The OGS has 30 branches throughout the province that are not listed here. As well, there are a number of genealogical organizations, unaffiliated with OGS, located throughout the province.

Société franco-ontarienne d'histoire et de généalogie
C.P. 8254 — Succursale T
Ottawa, ON K1G 3H7
Tel: 613-729-5769
Fax: [none noted]
laurentian.ca/sfohg
The Société franco-ontarienne has many branches throughout Ontario; contact the provincial group for the address of the branch in your area of interest.

Prince Edward Island Genealogical Society (PEIGS)
Box 2744
Charlottetown, PE C1A 8C4
Telephone/Fax: [none noted]
<www.islandregister.com/peigs.html
Maintains a library and issues a journal: P.E.I. Genealogical Society, Inc Newsletter
The Province of Quebec has the largest number of individual genealogical groups, most of which are affiliated with the provincial federation. They are not listed here individually. The major English and French-speaking societies are listed below.

Fédération québecoise des sociétés de généalogie
C.P. 9454
Sainte-Foy, QC G1V 4A8
Tel: 418-651-9127
Fax: 418-651-2643
www.federationgenealogie.qc.ca

Quebec Family History Society
Box 1026
Pointe Claire, QC H9S 4H9
Tel: 514-695-1502
www.cam.org/~qfhs/index.html
[This is the English-speaking society]

Société de généalogie de Québec
C. P. 9066
Sainte-Foy, QC G1V 4A8
Tel: 418-651-9127
Fax: 418-651-2643
www.genealogie.org.club/sgq/
[This is the major French-speaking society]

Société de généalogie de l'Outaouais
C.P. 2025, Succursale B
Hull, QC J8X 3Z2
Tel: 819-772-3010
Fax: [none noted]
www3.sympatico.ca/sgo/

Saskatchewan Genealogical Society (SGS)
2nd floor, 1870 Lorne Street, Regina
mailing address: Box 1894
Regina, SK S4P 3E1
Tel: 306-780-9207
Fax: 306-781-6021
www.saskgenealogy.com/
The Saskatchewan Genealogical Society has a number of branches throughout the province that are not listed here; check the Web site.

Yukon Territory Genealogical Society at the Dawson City Museum and Historical Society
Box 303
Dawson City, YT Y0B 1G0
Tel: 867-993-5291
Fax: [none noted]
users.yknet.yk.ca/dcpages/Museum.html

Endnotes

1   Ottawa: DIAND, 1978.

2   Veterans' Land Act, S.C., 1942, (6 George VI, c. 33); R.S.C. 1970, c. V-4, [and variously amended since].

3   For the early history of school establishment among the Indian communities see J. D. Wilson, "'No Blanket to be Worn in School': The Education of Indians in Nineteenth-Century Ontario" in *Indian Education in Canada, Volume 1: The Legacy*, J. Barman, Y. Hebert, D. McCaskill, editors (Vancouver: University of British Columbia Press, 1986).

4   For a discussion of Indian policy in the Atlantic colonies see L. F. S. Upton, *Micmacs and Colonists: Indian White Relations in the Maritimes 1713–1867* (Vancouver: University of British Columbia Press, 1979).

5   An Act for the better protection of the lands and property of the Indians in Lower Canada, S.C., 1850, (13 & 14 Victoria, c. 42). Reproduced in Gail Hinge, *Consolidation of Indian Legislation*, 2 vols. (Ottawa: DIAND, 1975?) p. 87.

6   Leslie and Maguire, *The Historical Development of the Indian Act*, pp. 23–26.

7   An Act to encourage the gradual civilization of the Indian Tribes in this Province, and to amend the Laws respecting Indians. S.C., 1857, (20 Victoria, c. 26). Reproduced in Hinge, p. 114. See also Leslie and Maguire, pp. 26–28.

8   See Leslie and Maguire. See also *Indian Acts and Amendments, 1868–1950*, 2nd edition (Ottawa: DIAND, 1981).

9   For additional information on the mandate of GAD, see the LAC Web site **www. collectionscanada.ca**

10   *Corporate Archival Control Manual* (Ottawa: Library and Archives Canada, 2004), Appendix C (Glossary), p.6.

11   Bill Russell, "The White Man's Paper Burden: Aspects of Records Keeping in the Department of Indian Affairs, 1860–1914," *Archivaria* 19 (Winter 1984–85). For the post-War period see RG 10, vol. 8586, file 1/1-6-3.

12   Access to Information and Privacy Legislation is composed of two parts: The Access to Information Act, R.S.C. 1985, c. A-1; and The Privacy Act, R.S.C. 1985, c. P-21, both variously amended to date.

[13] *Guidelines for the Disclosure of Personal Information for Historical Research at the Library and Archives Canada* (Ottawa: Library and Archives Canada, 1995). p. 1.

[14] Ibid.

[15] (Ottawa: DIAND, 1990)

[16] Ibid

[17] See *Contemporary Indian Legislation, 1951-1978* (Ottawa: DIAND, 1981).

[18] *Fourth Census of Canada 1901* (Ottawa: Kings Printer, 1902), p. xv

[19] RG 10, vol. 2520, file 107000, pt. 7

[20] RG 10, vol. 3161, file 365009-1

[21] RG 10, vol. 6823, file 494-16-5; RG 10, vol. 3161, files 365009-1, 365009-2A, 365009-3, and 365009-4

[22] See, for example, the comments of R. H. Coats, 13 April 1916 in RG 10, vol. 6823, file 494-16-5

[23] RG 10, vol. 6823, file 494-16-5

[24] RG 10, vol. 3161, file 365009-3

[25] See page 8 for references to such "census" lists for Upper Canada and Lower Canada. See also RG 10, vol.2520, file 107000X for census returns for selected Ontario bands, 1856-1866. These latter records are not full nominal censuses but name head of household only, with numbers of other family members.

[26] What would be an amusing sidelight, if its implications were not so serious, is an exchange of memoranda in 1910 among Supervisor of Statistics, J. A. Macrae; Assistant Secretary, S. Stewart; and DSGIA, F. Pedley, in which the latter ordered his staff to publish incorrect figures in the 1910 *Annual Report* because he did not want a drastic decrease in the population from the previous year to be shown. The possible bad publicity from too great a drop in numbers, it would seem, was more than the deputy minister could bear to countenance (RG 10, vol. 3159, file 358999-1).

[27] Circular of 13 March 1886, RG 10, vol. 2298, file 59268.

[28] See, for example, the census of the Mississaugas of Mud Lake and Rice Lake for 1885 (which includes named head of household, number of family members with children grouped by age and gender) in RG 10, vol. 2298, file 59268; the nominal lists for those bands under agent Van Abbott in the Northern Superintendency, 1875, in RG 10, vol. 1970, file 5354; the lists (head of household, gender and number of family members by age group and religion) for the Micmac of Annapolis and Shelburne, 1900, in RG 10, vol. 2520, file 107006, pt. 6; and the nominal list of Shelburne Micmac, 1901, in RG 10, vol. 2520, file, 107006, pt. 7, as in the illustration on p10.

Full nominal censuses (name, age, gender) for the Columbia Lake, Lower Kootenay, Shuswap, St. Marys and Tobacco Plain reserves for 1944, and a full nominal census (name, age, gender, religion, civil status) for 1944 of the Abenakis of Odanak are found in what otherwise is a general file about the taking of the DIA census (RG 10, vol. 2799, file 160370, pt. 5). A similar, seemingly general, file (RG 10, vol. 2799, file 160370, pt. 1) contains full nominal census returns for 1923 for the Tahltan Band and Nelson River Nomads of Northern British

Columbia and the Wood Mountain Band; a partial nominal census (name of adults only and numbers and ages of children) for the Natashquan, Romain, and St.Augustin communities (Quebec) for 1929; and a 1936 return for the Nemaska, Neoskweskan and Mistassini bands of Quebec (head of family named with gender and number of others).

See also RG 10, vol. 2799, file 160370, pt. 4 for 1939-1940 returns (some full nominal and some with names of household head only) for the Kootenay Agency bands, the Middle River reserve, Prince Edward Island reserves, Onion Lake and Meadow Lake Agencies (Saskatchewan).

29 Circular of 1 May 1939, RG 10, vol. 2799, file 160370, pt. 4.

30 Geo. W. Burbidge to L. Vankoughnet, 7 March 1885, RG 10, vol. 2291, file 58063.

31 RG 10, vol. 3087, file 279222-1B.

32 See W. C. Laidlaw to DIA, 26 January 1914, and J. D. McLean's reply of 2 February 1914, RG 10, vol. 4057, file 388217.

33 Ibid., D. MacKie to DIA, 29 January 1920, and McLean's reply of 6 March 1920.

34 Circular to all British Columbia agents, 21 September 1916, RG 10, vol. 3086, file 279222-1A.

35 See memo of H. W. McGill, Director, IAB, to the Deputy Minister, 28 March 1939, RG 10, vol. 2799, file 160370, pt. 4.

36 A small selection of registers and records of births and deaths survives for a few Saskatchewan and British Columbia bands in RG 10, vols. 9994-9995, 9997, 10001 and 10006 as well as scattered among field office series. See, for example, the unprocessed Accession 1990-91/026 of records transferred from the Ontario Regional office of DIAND, but which includes material from the now closed Peterborough and Kingston District offices such as vital statistics records for Golden Lake Agency, 1858-1937, and Tyendinaga marriage and death registers from the 1930s and 1940s.

37 An excellent analysis of the content of a typical paylist (with an illustration) is provided in Bennett McCardle, *Indian History and Claims: A Research Handbook*, vol. 1, pp. 148-149.

38 See, for example, the files from the DIA file classification block 28-3 (annuity) in RG 10, vols. 6878-6923, or from the 58 block and 28-4 block (interest distribution) in RG 10, vols. 7944-7957 and 8114-8129, respectively. For similar records from an earlier period in the West see the Black Series, RG 10, vols. 3969-3980.

39 See, for example, the records of membership from the 62 block (a block from the DIA's old First Series file classification system) now found in RG 10, vols. 7957-7976. Similar files from the 3-3 block in the successor DIA file classification system are found among the band management records now in RG 10, vols. 7101-7159. Membership files will also be found scattered through the Red and Black series and may be identified in the finding aids by such file titles as "membership" and "admission to/discharge from treaty." For commutations see the records of the 28-8 block in RG 10, vols. 8156-8173.

40 See, for example, the individual enfranchisement case files from the 8000 and 8100 blocks of the DIA's old Thousand Series file classification system in RG 10, vols. 7195-7324, or those from the 37-3 block of the successor DIA file classification system now found in the microfilmed case files series in RG 10 (microfilm reels M-2521 to M-2777).

41 See, for example, the series of Maritime field office enfranchisement files scattered throughout RG 10, vols. 8324-8386.

[42]   See the series of microfilmed case files in RG 10 (reels M-2521 to M-2777).

[43]   RG 10, vols. 9973-9985.

[44]   See trapline registration files for the 1930s and 1940s in the records of the Office of the Indian Commissioner for British Columbia found in RG 10, vols. 11290-11294.

[45]   See RG 10, vols. 11819-11820 for loan applications. For individual case files see the 19-7 block records in microfilmed case files in the Headquarters central registry system series in RG 10, reels M-2521 to M-2777.

[46]   For general files from the DIA's 19 block of economic development records see, for example, RG 10, vols. 6943-6952 and 7982-7994. For field office holdings see, for example, the 19-7 block of Maritime field office case files scattered through RG 10, vols. 8324-8386.

[47]   RG 10, vols. 11811-11818.

[48]   RG 10, vols. 7338-7458.

[49]   RG 10, Accession V-1988-89/206, boxes 9-10.

[50]   RG 10, vols. 6835-6857, 8190-8193.

[51]   RG 10, vols. 6923-6942, 8194-8211, 8387-8393.

[52]   RG 10, vols. 7093-7101.

[53]   Among the headquarters miscellaneous records there is a series relating to the enrolment of Indians into the program for allowances for the aged. RG 10, vols. 11885-11895 include application forms for these allowances which include such information as birth date and maiden name of women. The application forms are arranged by province and according to a numbering system based on date of receipt and are not nominally indexed.

[54]   See RG 10, vols. 7464-7476. There are a few murder case files in the Headquarters central registry system microfilmed case files (RG 10, reels M-2521 to M-2777) filed under the subject block 37-7 "Miscellaneous Cases." These latter records are subject to ATIP review prior to the release of information.

[55]   RG 10, vols. 7978-81, 8848-70.

[56]   See, for example, the extensive blocks of general education files in RG 10, vols. 8753-8810 and 7180-7194. As an example of the type of individual-level information which may be found on a general file see RG 10, vol. 6200, file 466-1, pts. 1-5 (Six Nations-Mohawk Institute, 1921-1949). Included in the general correspondence about school operations, curriculum, and building maintenance are such items as: a nominal return of "orphaned and neglected children" in attendance in 1921; the principal's quarterly reports which include particulars of individual pupils, especially in the section concerning student health; a long memorandum detailing careers of "successful graduates"; an extended correspondence with a lawyer regarding punishment meted out to a pupil; and a number of teacher application forms.

[57]   See, for example, the block of admissions and discharges files for residential schools, Canada-wide, c.1953-1968, in RG 10, vols. 6857-6877.

[58]   See, for example, the series of quarterly returns for residential schools, Canada-wide, 1951-68, in RG 10, vols. 8993-9001, or the individual school quarterly returns in the Schools Files sub-series. As an example, see the illustration on page 32.

59   See, for example, the Principal's Monthly Report (PMR) records scattered throughout RG 10, vols. 8438-74, for the 1950s and 1960s.

60   For an example of the type of education record maintained at an agency/district office, see the records of the Chapleau and Sault Ste. Marie agencies which include daily attendance records, some dating to 1916 (RG 10, vols. 10789-10792), or the similar record for the Cecilia Jeffrey Indian School, Kenora Agency, 1919-1954 (RG 10, vol. 11214) and the Mamalillikulla Day School, 1951-1962, and the Quatsino Day School, Campbell River District, 1954-1956 (RG 10, vol. 11188). Those researching this type of record are also directed to the unprocessed accessions in NA custody and especially those in the Pacific Region Federal Records Centre. See, for example, the records of the Kuper Island Residential School, 1941-1949, in Accession V-1984-85/316 or those of the Crosby Girls' School, 1916-1935, in Accession V-1988-89/206. See also the Alnwick and Rama schools registers from the 1950s and 1960s and the school attendance register for a number of Ontario schools from the 1930s and 1940s in Accession 1990-91/026 at LAC headquarters.

61   See McCardle, *Indian History and Claims*, p. 315.

62   See *Indian Acts and Amendments 1868-1950.*

63   RG 10, vol. 6829, file 503-4-2

64   RG 10, vols. 3180-3182, file 452124 (various parts).

65   RG 10, vols. 6762-6806. See, as examples, the illustrations on page 36.

66   For the Office of the ICBC see RG 10, vols. 11288-11290. For the Kwawkewlth Agency see RG 10, Vols. 11154-11155. There is also one file from this agency relating to World War I, including enlistments (RG 10, vol. 11154, file Shannon C.R. 34).

67   Soldier Settlement Act, S.C., 1919, (9-10 George V, c. 71)

68   RG 10, vol. 11884. The accounting records of disbursements from and repayments to the Soldier Settlement Fund are found among the Trust Fund ledgers in account #455 which was set aside for this purpose.

69   RG 10, vols. 7484-7536.

70   See Veterans' Land Act, R.S.C., 1970, c. V-4, [and variously amended to 1997].

71   These are scattered through RG 10, vols. 8324-8386 and identified by the file classification block number 39-6.

72   See Terry Cook, *Sources for the Study of the Canadian North* (Ottawa: Public Archives of Canada, 1980). There are scattered records of contact with the Inuit communities in RG 10 but these are not easily located. See, for example, the 1917 census returns of "Indians and Eskimos" provided by Hudson's Bay Company agents from various posts along James and Hudson's Bay in RG 10, vol. 6823, file 494-16-5. These records provide name of family head and numbers of men, women, and children in each family.

73   See James F. Kidd, "Polar Archives: Thematic Guide," and "Post-Confederation Sources Relating to Indians and Inuit: Thematic Guide," both unpublished finding aids in the Manuscript Division, Library and Archives Canada. See also the comments in Bennett McCardle's thematic guide.

74   See *Indian Act and Amendments 1868-1950.*

75 See, for example, RG 10, vols. 3724-3725, files 24303-2A, 24303-3, and 24303-4 which contain correspondence regarding "half-breeds" in Manitoba and the Northwest Territories withdrawing from treaty, and correspondence relating to requests for treaty admission or discharge, 1886-1900; RG 10, vol. 3723, files 24303-1 and 24303-2 concerning notification of withdrawal of several "half-breed" women, 1885-1887; RG 10, vol. 3775, files 37267-1 and 37267-2, with correspondence regarding "half-breeds" who have withdrawn from treaty but not received scrip, 1887-1894, and regarding those now wishing to re-enter treaty, 1895-1900; RG 10, vol. 4020, file 281180, general correspondence regarding claims for scrip from Manitoba "half-breeds," 1905-1932; and RG 10, vols. 3587-3594, file 1239 (many parts) regarding applications for withdrawal of "half-breeds" from treaty, 1885-1926. One especially important block of records is a series of admission to/discharge from treaty files in RG 10, vols. 3996-3999, files 206070-1 to 206070-36. The various parts of this file relate each to a different agency in Manitoba, Saskatchewan, and Alberta. Outside dates for the block are 1894-1917.

The taking of scrip is largely an issue involving the Aboriginal people of the Prairie provinces. The option of scrip instead of treaty was not made available to the Aboriginal people who negotiated Treaty 9 in Northern Ontario in 1905/6. See RG 10, vol. 3093, file 289300 concerning the petition of certain "half-breeds" of Moose Factory for scrip and/or consideration and applications to be placed on the paylists, 1905-1910.

76 RG 10, vol. 10037 provides name of family head, band number, date of discharge; RG 10, vol. 10038 provides name of family head, band number, and agency; RG 10, vol. 10039 provides information on a number of individual cases setting out details such as births and deaths and payments under treaty; RG 10, vol. 10040 is a register of 867 applications arranged by date of application, not by name, providing name of family head, date of application receipt (and in some entries very full citations of related correspondence), band number, and remarks (for example, discharge date, refusal to discharge and reasons).

77 *Civil Service List: ...*, Ottawa: Parliament/Secretary of State, 1886?- [annual]

78 *Annual Report*. Most government departments issue a report to Parliament on an annual basis, many of which were published and made available to the public.

79 RG 10, vols. 9178-9187.

80 In the arcane world of turn of the century DIA staffing, these terms designated a different status of employment as well as, generally, a different location of employment (although you could be an officer of the Inside service but operate outside DIA HQ). For many years, appointment to the Outside service necessitated the passage of an Order-in-Council that, of course, offers another LAC source (RG 2) for documenting the details of an appointment.

81 The files cited are found, respectively, as follows: RG 10, vol. 2114, file 21376; RG 10, vol. 2170, file 35612; RG 10, vol. 2378, file 77020; RG 10, vol. 3177, file 444356.

82 See, for example, RG 10, vol. 6826, file 497-1-1. For this kind of flavour even the seemingly trivial file can be of interest. Files relating to office procedures and the "departmental orders" files (RG 10, vol. 2277, files 55412-1 and 55412-2) which contain copies of memoranda that would have circulated among the staff about such things as hours of work, work habits, and office discipline, give quite an insight into working conditions.

83 See, for example, RG 10, vols. 5991-5992 for reports on Indian schools on Ontario reserves, 1894-1900. These are, in fact, reports made by the inspectors of the provincial Department of Education who were responsible in this period for inspecting both Indian reserve and provincial schools. Inspection reports from the twentieth century (by no means a complete collection) will be found among the central registry files (subject block 23 — Reports and Returns — in RG 10, vols. 8438-8474).

84 See RG 10, vols. 6003-6004, file 1-1-1x, parts 7-14, covering the period 1942-1954. These records include written teacher applications, letters of recommendation, correspondence regarding qualifications, and many application forms on which are recorded tombstone data as well as academic and professional qualifications.

85 On Scott's career in the DIA, see the excellent study by E. Brian Titley, *A Narrow Vision: Duncan Campbell Scott and the Administration of Indian Affairs in Canada* (Vancouver: University of British Columbia Press, 1986) which, by the author's own admission, is not intended to be a biography of Scott but a study of his public service career. There are a small number of biographical studies which have focused on the careers of individuals in the DIA and which have relied to an extent on RG 10 as a source. See, for example, David Hall, "Clifford Sifton and Canadian Indian Administration, 1896-1905," *Prairie Forum* 2, nos. 1-2 (1977); Douglas Leighton, "A Victorian Civil Servant at Work: Laurence Vankoughnet and the Canadian Indian Department, 1874-1893," in I. A. L. Getty and A. S. Lussier, eds. *As Long As the Sun Shines and the Water Flows* (Vancouver: University of British Columbia Press, 1983); Jean Larmour's two studies of Edgar Dewdney and his role as Indian Commissioner in the West in *Saskatchewan History*, 23 (1970) and 33 (1980); and A. J. Looy, "Saskatchewan's First Indian Agent, M. G. Dickieson," *Saskatchewan History*, 32 (1979).

86 For a short summary of the history leading up to the Royal Proclamation of 1763, see Peter A. Cumming and Neil H. Mickenberg, *Native Rights in Canada*, 2nd edition (Toronto: Indian-Eskimo Association of Canada and General Publishing Co. Ltd., 1972), pp. 26-30.

87 See the comments in J. E. Hodgetts, *Pioneer Public Service: An Administrative history of the United Canadas, 1841-1867* (Toronto: n.p., 1955), p. 220.

88 See RG 10, vol. 712, Abstract of Petitions, 1834-1844 which records name and residence of petitioner, date of petition, and abstract of content. Arranged alphabetically by name of petitioner, these are largely land-related petitions from both non-Indians and Indians. RG 10, vol. 713 contains Abstracts of Petitions, Upper Canada, 1844-1850. Here the petition abstracts are arranged chronologically with a nominal index. The petitions themselves are found in RG 10, vols. 120-123 and cover the years 1840-1850.

89 See RG 10, vol. 103, Six Nations Grand River Claims, 1788-1844; and RG 10, vol. 762, Six Nations Alpha Nominal Index to Grand River Claims.

90 RG 10, vol. 726, Upper Canada Inspection Returns, 1833-1842; and RG 10, vols. 727-735, Canada West Inspection Returns, 1835-1869, see the illustration on page 50.

91 See RG 10, vols. 6616-6730.

92 See the 32 block files scattered among the land records in RG 10, vols. 7995-8096.

93 See, for example, the small block of lease files from the 1940s from the New Westminster and Cowichan agencies in British Columbia in the records of the office of the Indian Commissioner for British Columbia in RG 10, vols. 11050-11051.

Glossary

There is an excellent glossary in Bennett McCardle's *Indian History and Claims: A Research Handbook* (Ottawa, Ont.: DIAND, 1982). The terms listed below are meant only as a quick reference. For other, or more exact definitions, it is suggested that you examine Bennett McCardle's book.

Aboriginal people   The various peoples indigenous to the Americas before the arrival of the Europeans; or any persons descended from those first inhabitants. Indians, Inuit and Métis are identified as the Aboriginal peoples of Canada in the Constitution Act of 1982, Sec. 35 (2).

Access to Information and Privacy Legislation   Those laws enacted by the federal government that guarantee access to information (collected by the government) by the public, but which also protect the privacy of the individual under certain circumstances.

active records   Those records necessary for conducting the current business of a department that therefore must be maintained in the office that created them. The age of the records has no bearing on whether they are active or inactive; a historical record, which one might assume should be in an archive, might still be active.

annual report   A document prepared annually to report on the activities of a department, agency or individual for the preceding year. All departments must report to Parliament on an annual basis and most of these reports are published.

annuity   An annual payment made by the Crown, from Parliamentary appropriation, to First Nations treaty signatories and their descendants, according to the terms of the treaty they and/or their ancestors signed. Prior to the inauguration of the Indian Register (c.1951), the paylists that the DIA officers created to document this fulfilment of a treaty obligation, were frequently used as a record of whom the government recognized as having Indian status. As such, treaty annuity paylists are often consulted in genealogical research.

archives   are 1) the non-current records of an organization or institution preserved because of their continuing historical value; also referred to as archival materials or archival holdings, or 2) the building where such materials are located, also referred to as an archival repository.

Archives Branch, Department of Agriculture   The forerunner of the Public Archives of Canada (PAC), later named the Library and Archives Canada (LAC).

Atlantic Canada   The area that includes New Brunswick, Newfoundland, Nova Scotia and Prince Edward Island. The term Maritime Provinces does not include Newfoundland.

BMDs   A term used by genealogists for the vital records of births [or baptisms], marriages and deaths [or interments] collected by the government or found in church registers. Sometimes referred to as "tombstone" information.

Band, the   "a group of Indian people. The word has at least two meanings today: 1) a legal group defined by the Indian Act. In this sense, a Band is the basic unit of Indian government recognized by the federal government…; 2) a small social group, usually of people following a traditional life of hunting, fishing, trapping and gathering, with special kinds of kinship and family patterns". (McCardle: Vol. 2, p.302)

Band council   "the governing body of a band under the Indian Act. It is composed of one or more Chiefs, and usually several Councillors (formerly called "headmen"). Some bands choose their councils under the elective system, and some by custom." (McCardle: Vol. 2, p.302)

band membership   The right to belong to a given Indian band bestowed by the Band council itself; usually connected to being a status Indian.

bureaucracy   Government by a central administration; officialism or those officials acting for such a government.

Black Series   The name given by the DIA to its headquarters central registry file classification system for files relating to Western Canada, and in use during the late-nineteenth/early twentieth centuries. Name apparently derived from the colour of the covers of the books initially used to register correspondence.

British North America   That area of land in North America originally settled by, and under the control of, the British. It included the Hudson's Bay territories in the far north, the Atlantic provinces, and the 13 American colonies. In 1763, France ceded New France (Québec and what is now present-day Ontario) to Britain. This area later became known as The Canadas. In 1783, the 13 American colonies were ceded to the United States of America after the Treaty of Paris was signed.

Canadas, The   was the land area ceded by France to Britain, in 1763, after the fall of New France. The area first became known as Western and Eastern Québec and was later renamed Upper Canada and Lower Canada in 1791. In 1841, under Act of Union, Upper and Lower Canada were again renamed Canada East and Canada West, and united to become the Province of Canada.

case files   Files and records created about one specific individual, around one specific subject area; a group of files kept together each containing the activities of one person.

census records   Those records kept by the government when it officially counted the population within the country; usually done every ten years, hence called a decennial census.

Chief   The head of an Indian band, tribe or clan; the position can be either hereditary or, more often, now elected by the band.

Civil Service List   A list published each year that catalogues the names of the employees of the federal government and giving the department of employment, position and other information.

Claims and Historical Research Centre, DIAND   A resource centre (formerly known as the Treaties and Historical Research Centre) within the Department which gathers, and makes available to researchers, information relating to claims and historical research as it relates to the Department and its records. Staff of the Centre have also, historically, both prepared and commissioned historical studies relating to DIAND and, in particular, treaties and claims. The Centre is also the office in DIAND headquarters that one contacts initially in order to arrange to consult records still in the custody of DIAND.

Colonies, The A settlement in a new country forming a community fully or partially subject to the mother state; the term the British government used for its possessions overseas, as in the 13 Colonies in North America.

commutation "a legal action provided for in the Indian Act between 1876 and 1951. An Indian woman who married a non-Indian, and so lost her Indian status, could 'wind up' her financial connection with the band by 'taking commutation'. This is, she received a lump-sum payment covering ten years' worth of a) Treaty annuities and b) any other regular cash payments made out of the band's trust fund. If she did not 'commute her interest' in this way, she could continue to collect these monies indefinitely. Her name remained on band lists for the purpose of recording the payments, but she had no other rights as an Indian." (McCardle: Vol. 2, p.304)

Confederation The politically joining together of the then Province of Canada, New Brunswick and Nova Scotia under the British North America Act in 1867. Over the years the other provinces joined in to make up the Dominion of Canada: Manitoba (1870); British Columbia (1871); Prince Edward Island (1873); Alberta and Saskatchewan (1905); and, finally, Newfoundland and Labrador (1949).

current records See active records

custody Refers to the guardianship of records, archives and manuscripts that includes both the physical responsibility and the legal responsibility for them; can also refer to the guardianship of children and individuals.

decennial census See census records

Deputy Superintendent General of Indian Affairs A position carried over into the post-Confederation period of an office created in 1862 in the Province of Canada and, throughout the period 1867-1936, the senior public servant in the Indian Affairs administration carried this title and was what would be called, today, a deputy minister of a federal government department. The term was also in use during the years 1794-1828 to describe a position in the Indian Department subordinate to that of the Superintendent General during the period of imperial control of Indian Affairs.

document 1) recorded information regardless of its medium or characteristics (often used interchangeably with record); or 2) a single record or manuscript item.

Eastern Canada The area of Canada east from the Manitoba-Ontario border to the Maritimes.

electronic data files Files produced by computer technology that can be found on tape or disc. The long-term stability of the medium is not yet known although they are being preserved in archives.

enfranchisement The voluntary or involuntary loss of Indian status, originally symbolized by the taking of the franchise, that is, the right to vote. That right was denied status Indians for many years because they were considered to be akin to legal minors and wards of the state. By enfranchising, or taking the franchise, Indians renounced their legal status as wards of the state and accepted the full responsibility of citizenship.

Eskimo   See Inuit

establishment books   A series of DIA records, now in LAC custody in RG 10, maintained, originally, to keep track of salary paid to the DIA 'establishment' (the people in the employ of the Department). These are useful for the family historian as they provide detail of positions held and salaries paid, as well as some tombstone information and, frequently, a reference to the individual's personnel file.

field office   An office away from the central headquarters which covers a specific territory and responsibility. *See also* Regional Office.

finding aids   The descriptive media, published and unpublished, created by an archival agency or manuscript repository, to establish physical or administrative and intellectual control over records and other holdings. Basic finding aids include guides, inventories or registers, calendars, card catalogues, shelf and box lists, etc.

First Nations   Aboriginal peoples or communities; sometimes, those specific groups considered by the Federal government to have "Indian status" under the Indian Act.

fonds   "the whole of the archival records, regardless of form or medium, automatically and organically created and/or accumulated and used by a particular individual, family or corporate body in the course of that creator's activities and functions."

Government Archives Division   That division of the Library and Archives Canada responsible for the appraisal, selection, custody and specialized reference of the unpublished historical records of the government of Canada. Its mandate includes all textual (paper), micrographic and electronic records created by the federal government judged to have archival or historical value.

half-breed   An English term used to denote people of mixed Aboriginal and white blood. Originally it was strictly a descriptive term, but gradually it acquired a pejorative meaning. *See also* Métis.

headquarters   The central office of the DIA (DIAND) in Ottawa which had control of the policies relating to the Native peoples.

Imperial government   The government in England that governed British North America before Confederation when Canada became a country.

Indian   The name first applied to the indigenous people of America by all Europeans — a misnomer due to the mistaken belief by Columbus that he had reached the Asiatic Indies in 1492, when he actually landed in the West Indies. Used by some Aboriginal people (other than Inuit or Métis) when speaking of themselves in English. Formerly used for people having legal status under the Federal Indian Act and who are now called "First Nations."

Indian census   The census taken by the DIA for its own information; often not a nominal census.

Indian Department of the Imperial government   A department created 1755 that lasted until 1860; it was responsible for dealing with the Indians in British North America through the governor of the various colonies.

Indian Land Registry   A registry maintained at DIAND headquarters under the direction of the Land Registrar. The Indian Act requires that the federal government, through DIAND, operate an Indian Land Registry where all documents granting or claiming an interest in Indian reserve land must registered and deposited. The Indian Land Registry performs for Indian reserve lands an equivalent function to that performed by provincial land registry offices for nonreserve lands.

Indian Register   A centralized register created in 1951 to record the name of every person who is entitled to be registered as an Indian.

Indian Economic Development Fund   A program and funding arrangement established by DIAND to provide loans, loan guarantees and grants to First Nations to promote economic development. Established in 1970, the program was phased out during the early 1990s.

Indigenous people   The people living in the country before the Europeans came to this continent; its Aboriginal peoples.

Inter-Institutional Loan   See Inter-Library loan

Inter-Library Loan (ILL)   A system that allows materials owned by one institution to be borrowed by an individual or another institution but which can only be used within the borrowing institution. That institution is responsible for the safe use of the borrowed material. Started by libraries to allow one library to borrow from another, it has since extended to archives, museums, etc.

Inuit   The Aboriginal peoples of the Arctic and Sub-Arctic; formerly known as "Eskimo" in English.

inventory   A basic archival finding aid that generally includes a brief history and function of the agency whose records are being described; a descriptive list of each record series giving, at minimum, such data as title, inclusive dates, quantity, arrangement, relationship to other series and significant subject content.

location ticket   Synonymous with "Certificate of Possession" defined in the Indian Act as documentary evidence of an Indian's right to use and occupy reserve lands pursuant to the provisions of subsection 20 (2) of the Act. Historically, the DIA issued a "location ticket" to an Indian who had a right to use and occupy a particular parcel of reserve land. Prior to the 1951 changes to the Indian Act, an Indian holding such a ticket was known as a "locatee," the land in question called a "location," and the document was a "location ticket."

Lower Canada   See Canadas, The

Manuscript Division   The name formerly used at Library and Archives Canada to describe the organizational unit that acquires and preserves private textual and electronic records of national significance.

manuscript group (MG)   Prior to the introduction of the *fonds* concept for archival description, Library and Archives Canada arranged and described its private textual record holdings according to "manuscript groups." In this system a manuscript group is an artificial grouping that brings *fonds* together by provenance (origin), subject or time period.

Maritime Provinces   The three east coast provinces of New Brunswick, Nova Scotia, and Prince Edward Island.

membership   See Band membership

Métis   Persons and communities of mixed Aboriginal and white descent, especially in the Canadian Northwest. Formerly used more narrowly for and by the descendants of the historic eighteenth- and nineteenth-century mixed blood Plains and Great Lakes communities. (French from the Latin *miscere*, "mixed." The English equivalent is half-breed.)

National Registration   An outcome of the National Resources Mobilization Act enacted in 1940 at the beginning World War II, which Act allowed the federal government to register all people in Canada for the war effort, British subjects and aliens alike, from age sixteen and up; an excellent genealogical resource.

Native   A collective word formerly used for all Aboriginal peoples, including First Nations, Métis and Inuit; now infrequently used.

non-status Indians   Persons and communities of mixed Aboriginal/non-Aboriginal descent; narrowly referring to people not granted status by the Federal government under the Indian Act.

Old Northwest   A term used by some historians to describe an area falling roughly within the confines of the present-day American Midwest and which includes the area contested between British and American authorities between the time of the signing of the Treaty of Paris (1783) — which assigned the territory to the United States — and the withdrawal of the last British troops as a consequence of the signing of the Jay Treaty in 1794.

patent   A written document from the government conferring a right or title on an individual for a piece of property obtained from that government; used more often during the nineteenth century with the granting of Crown Lands.

paylists   The lists prepared every year when the government granted gifts or monies to the various Indian bands.

Peace of 1783   Refers to the Treaty of Paris, completed in 1783, that ceded the 13 colonies and other lands to the United States after the American Revolutionary War.

Province of Canada   *See* Canadas, The

quinquennial census   A census taken every five years, rather than ten.

record group (RG)   Comprised of a body of historical records of the Federal government, from a single agency or a branch of the government that exhibited administrative continuity over a period of time now in the custody of the Library and Archives Canada.

record series   File units arranged in accordance with a filing system or maintained as a unit because they relate to a particular subject or function, or because of some other relationship arising out of their creation or use.

record sub-series   An aggregate of file units within a record series readily separated in terms of physical class, type, form, subject, or filing arrangement.

Red series   Name given by the DIA to its headquarters central registry file classification system for files relating to Eastern Canada. In use by the Department during the late-nineteenth/early twentieth centuries. Apparently derived from the colour of the covers of the books initially used to register correspondence.

Red ticket woman   An Indian women identified by the colour of a special card issued by the government to show that they continued to be Treaty Indians even though they had lost their status with the DIA as a Status Indian.

regional office   A type of field office. Usually a number of agency or district offices were subordinate to a Regional Office, which was itself subordinate to Headquarters. There are DIAND Regional Offices across the country today. The mandate and responsibilities of the Regional Offices have varied greatly over time.

reserve   Defined in the Indian Act as "a tract of land, the legal title to which is vested in Her Majesty, that has been set apart by Her Majesty for the use and benefit of a band."

residential schools   Schools established to teach the Indian children who were removed from the custody of their parents to reside in that institution.

School Files   A specific sub-series of the Headquarters central registry system series within RG 10, with outside dates of 1879-1953, the contents of which relate to the administration of schools for, and education of, status Indians. It is important to remember that all records in the School Files relate to education/schools, but not all records relating to schools and education in RG 10, for those dates, will be found in the School Files series.

scrip   *See* taking of scrip

series   *See* record series

Six Nations Allies   The Six Nations Indians who were, for the most part, allies of the British in the American Revolution, who, at the end of the war, were brought to Canada and settled in tracts of land primarily along the Grand River and at the Bay of Quinte in Ontario.

status Indian   *See* Indian

sub-series   *See* record sub-series

Superintendent of Indian Affairs   A position relating to Indian Affairs for the Imperial government, held first by Sir William Johnson and then by his successor, Colonel Guy Johnson. The position was re-named in 1782 as that of the Superintendent General of Indian Affairs.

Superintendent General of Indian Affairs   Essentially, the title given to the minister of the Crown responsible for Indian Affairs during the years 1868–1936. The office was created in 1868 by the passage of An Act providing for the organization of the Department of the Secretary of State of Canada and for the management of Indian and Ordnance lands, S.C., 1868, (31 Victoria, c. 42). The position was first held, ex officio, by the Secretary of State of Canada but, subsequently, was held by various other ministers of the Crown. The office was abolished in 1936. The term was also used in the period 1782–1828 and again in 1844–1860 to describe the position held by the senior officer in the Indian Administration in the British North American colonies.

taking of scrip   The act of accepting "scrip," which was a certificate issued to Métis families intended to compensate them for the loss of their Aboriginal rights and to deal with Métis grievances arising from the 1869-70 and 1885 uprisings. Scrip was redeemable in land or money, depending upon which scrip commission issued the scrip, and when. Historically, the fact that an Aboriginal person took scrip normally rendered them ineligible to participate in the benefits of Indian status.

tombstone information   The type of information found on a tombstone — birth, marriage and death dates. *See* BMDs and vital statistics records.

treaty   A formally concluded and ratified agreement between the government and persons that outlined provisions by which both sides are to abide.

treaty annuity paylists   Those documents created to record the fulfilment of the obligation made between the Crown and Canada's First Nations when the treaty included a stipulation for the annual payment of money — treaty annuities. These paylists were created at the time of payment when information about the numbers of Indians paid was recorded. The value of these records for genealogical research is the information they can provide about family structure.

In the earliest years, these paylists were not nominal but, frequently, one finds remarks that help explain family relationships and actions affecting individual status (for example, notes concerning marriage).

Treaty of Paris (1763)   The treaty signed in 1763 between France and Britain that ceded the area of New France to British rule.

Treaty of Paris (1783)   Also called the Peace of Versailles, the treaty signed in 1783 between Britain and the newly formed United States of America that ceded the 13 Colonies and other lands to the U.S.

treaty land entitlement   The land to which the signatories are entitled when that treaty contained a stipulation that a land base (a reserve) be set aside. The treaty provided a formula for the quantity of such land to be reserved, based upon population. This represents the treaty land entitlement of the signatories.

Upper Canada   The earlier name of Canada West.

vital stats   A slang term for the vital statistics records.

vital statistics records   The recordings of births, marriages and deaths maintained by the provinces that are an excellent source of genealogical information; before the various provincial Vital Statistics Acts were instituted, church registers and tombstone recordings must be used as the source of this information.

volume(s)   Containers of records.

Western Canada   The area of Canada west of the Manitoba-Ontario border towards British Columbia.

Bibliography and Further Reading

Canada. Parliamentary Legislation

Access to Information Act, R.S.C., 1985, c. A-1, and variously amended.

An Act for the better protection of the lands and property of the Indians in Lower Canada, S.C., 1850, (13 & 14 Victoria, c. 42), and now absorbed by the current legislation.

An Act for the gradual enfranchisement of Indians, the better management of Indian affairs, and to extend the provisions of the Act 31st Victoria, Chapter 42, S.C., 1869, (32-33 Victoria, c. 6), and now absorbed by the current legislation.

An Act to enact the Access to Information Act and the Privacy Act.... (29-30-31 Elizabeth II, c. 111, Schedule I and Schedule II) *See* Access to Information Act and the Privacy Act for the R.S.C. dates.

An Act to encourage the gradual civilization of the Indian Tribes in this Province, and to amend the Laws respecting Indians, S.C., 1857, (20 Victoria, c. 26), and now absorbed by the current legislation.

Indian Act, S.C., 1868, (31 Victoria, c. 42) referred to post-Confederation Acts of the provinces in terms of statutes 26, 31-35. This was amended in 1869 (32 Victoria, c. 6) and in 1874 (37 Victoria, c. 21) and re-enacted in 1876 (39 Victoria, c. 18) as the Consolidated Indian Act. A further re-enactment in 1880 (43 Victoria, c. 28) transferred responsibility for Indian affairs from the Secretary of State to the Minister of the Interior. The 1880 Act had important amendments, such as in 1884 (47 Victoria, cc. 27 & 28); and the revisions of 1886 (49 Victoria, c. 7); 1906 (6 Edward VII); and 1927 (6 George V). A new version was enacted in 1951 (15 George VI, c. 29). During this period, administration passed from Interior to Mines and Resources and then to Citizenship and Immigration. It was then placed under the Department of Indian Affairs and Northern Development, established by the Government Organization Act, 1966-67 (14-15 Elizabeth II, c. 25, ss. 15-21). Currently cited as Indian Act, R.S.C., 1985, c. I-5, and variously amended to 1996. *See* Statutes of Canada: consolidation prepared by the Department of Justice..., Vol.VII, Chapters I-1 to L-12.4 (Ottawa, Ont.: Supply and Services, 1993) and Canada Statute Citator, R.S.C. 1985, Vol.3 (Aurora, Ont.: Canada Law Book, 1998), pp. 13-5 to 13-28, both of which are available in most major public libraries.

Privacy Act, R.S.C., 1985, c. P-21, and variously amended.

Soldier Settlement Act, S.C., 1919, (9-10 George V, c. 71).

Veteran's Land Act, S.C., 1942, (6 George VI, c. 33); R.S.C., 1970, c. V-4, and variously amended.

Provincial Legislation

The Marriage Act and the Vital Statistics Act are not under federal jurisdiction but come under provincial legislation, therefore, these Acts were enacted at various times in the various Canadian provinces. *See* the Revised Statutes books issued, usually every ten years, by the provincial government(s) that interests you.

Books and Pamphlets

Alberta. Provincial Archives. Fact sheet: Indian and Métis search. Edmonton, Alta.: Provincial Archives of Alberta, n.d.

Allen, Robert S. *The British Indian Department and the Frontier in North America, 1755–1830.* Canadian Historic Sites, Occasional papers in archaeology and history: No 14, pp 5-125. Ottawa, Ont.: National Historic Parks and Sites Branch, Parks Canada and Department of Indian and Northern Affairs, 1975.

Allen, Robert S. *His Majesty's Indian Allies: British Indian Policy in the Defence of Canada, 1774–1815.* Toronto, Ont.: Dundurn Press, 1992.

Allen, Robert S. and Mary A.T. Tobin. *Native Studies in Canada: A Research Guide.* 3rd edition Ottawa, Ont.: Treaties and Historical Research Centre: Comprehensive Claims Branch, Department of Indian and Northern Affairs, 1989

Antone, Bob. *The Longhouse of One Family: A Kinship Model of the Iroquoian Clan System.* Brantford, Ont.: Woodland Indian Cultural Educational Centre, c1987.

Archives Association of Ontario, Communications Committee. *Directory of Archives in Ontario.* 2nd edition. Toronto, Ont.: Archives Association of Ontario, 1995. Now also at <aao.fis.utoronto.ca/Directory/DAIO.html>

Archives nationales du Québec. *Catalogue des fonds et collections d'archives d'origine privée: conservés au centre d'archives de Montréal, de Laval, de Lanaudierre, des Laurentides et de la Montérégie.* Québec, Qué,: Ministre des affaires culturelles, 1992.

Barman, Jean, Yvonne Hebert, Don McCaskill, editors. *Indian Education in Canada,* Vol.1: *The Legacy. Indian Education in Canada,* Vol.2: *The Challenge.* Nakoda Institute occasional papers, 2 & 3. Vancouver, B.C.: University of British Columbia Press, 1986-87.

Battiste, Marie Ann and Jean Barman, editors. *First Nations Education in Canada: The Circle Unfolds.* Vancouver, B.C.: University of British Columbia Press, 1995.

Baxter Angus. *Angus Baxter's Do's And Don'ts for Ancestor-Hunters.* Baltimore, Md.: Genealogical Publishing, 1988.

———. *In Search of Your Canadian Roots: Tracing Your Family Tree in Canada.* 2nd edition, revised & updated. Toronto, Ont.: Macmillan Canada, (1989) 1994; Baltimore, Md.: Genealogical Publishing, 1994.

———. *In Search of Your Roots: A Guide for Canadians Seeking Their Ancestors.* rev & updated. Toronto, Ont.: Macmillan Canada, (1978) (1984) 1991.

Canada: Department of Indian Affairs and Northern Development (DIAND). *Changes to the Indian Act…Resulting from the Passage of Bill C-31*. Ottawa, Ont.: DIAND, 1985.

———. *Contemporary Indian Legislation, 1951–1978*. Ottawa, Ont.: DIAND, (1981) 1984.

———. *Impacts of the 1985 Amendments to the Indian Act (Bill C-31): Summary Report*. Ottawa, Ont.: DIAND, 1990.

———. *Indian Acts and Amendments, 1868–1950*, 2nd edition. Ottawa, Ont.: DIAND, 1981.

———. "Indian Band membership: an information booklet concerning new Indian Band membership laws and the preparation of Indian Band membership codes." Ottawa, Ont.: DIAND, 1990.

———. *Schedule of Indian Bands, Reserves and Settlement Including Membership and Population Locations and Area in Hectares*. Ottawa, Ont.: DIAND, 1991.

Canada: Ministry of Supply and Services. *Guidelines for the Disclosure of Personal Information for Historical Research at the Library and Archives Canada*. Ottawa, Ont.: Ministry of Supply and Services, 1995.

Canada. Parliament. *Civil Service List: …* [annual]. Ottawa, Ont.: Parliament/Secretary of State, 1886?–

Canadian Institute for Historical Microreproductions (CIHM). *Native Studies Collection*, 2nd edition revised and updated. Ottawa, Ont.: CIHM, 1995

Carpenter, Cecilia S. *How to Research American Indian Blood Lines: A Manual on Indian Genealogical Research*. Orting, Wa.: Heritage Quest, 1987; Bountiful, UT.: American Genealogical Lending Library, 1991.

Cook, Terry. *Sources for the Study of the Canadian North*. Ottawa, Ont.: Public Archives of Canada, 1980.

Cumming, Peter A. *Indian Rights: A Century of Oppression*. Toronto, Ont.: Indian-Eskimo Association of Canada, [1969].

——— and Neil H. Mickenberg, co-editors. *Native Rights in Canada*, 2nd edition. Toronto, Ont.: Indian-Eskimo Association of Canada, 1972.

Dempsey, L. James. *Warriors of the King — Prairie Indians in World War I*. Regina: Canadian Plains Research Center, University of Regina, 1999.

Fenton, William N. *The Roll Call of the Iroquois Chiefs: A Study of a Mnemonic Cane from the Six Nations Reserve*. Washington, D.C.: Smithsonian Institution, 1950; Ohsweken, Ont.: Iroqrafts, 1983 reprint.

Faux, David K. *Understanding Ontario First Nations Genealogical Records: Sources and Cases*. Toronto: Ontario Genealogical Society, 2002.

Gaffen, Fred. *Forgotten Soldiers: An Illustrated History of Canada's Native Peoples in Both World Wars*. Penticton, B.C.: Theytus Books, 1984.

Graham, Elizabeth. *Medicine Man to Missionary: Missionaries As Agents of Change among the Indians of Southern Ontario, 1784–1867*. Toronto, Ont.: Peter Martin Associates, 1975.

Graymont, Barbara. *The Iroquois in the American Revolution*. Syracuse, N.Y.: Syracuse University Press, 1972.

Hinge, Gail. *Consolidation of Indian Legislation*, 2 vols. Ottawa, Ont.: Department of Indian and Northern Affairs, 1975?

Hives, Christopher, editor. *A Guide to Archival Repositories in British Columbia*. Vancouver, B.C.: Archives Association of British Columbia, 1992.

Hodgetts, J. E. *Pioneer Public Service: An Administrative History of the United Canadas, 1841–1867*. Toronto, Ont.: University of Toronto Press, 1955.

Jenness, Diamond. *The Indian Background of Canadian History*. National Museum of Canada Anthropological Series No.21. Ottawa, Ont.: J.O. Patenaude, 1937.

———. *The Indians of Canada*, 6th edition. National Museum of Canada Anthropological Series No.15. Ottawa, Ont.: Secretary of State, [1932] 1963. This edition has had numerous reprints.

Johnson, William, Sir. *The Papers of Sir William Johnson*. 14 vols. Albany, N.Y.: University of the State of New York, 1921-1957.

Johnston, Charles M., editor. *The Valley of the Six Nations: A Collection of Documents on the Indian Lands of the Grand River*. Toronto, Ont.: The Champlain Society, 1964.

Jonasson, Eric. *The Canadian Genealogical Handbook: A Comprehensive Guide to Finding Your Ancestors in Canada*, 2nd ed. rev. & enlarged. Winnipeg, Man.: Wheatfield Press, 1978.

Kidd, James F. "Polar Archives: Thematic Guide." (Unpublished finding aid available for consultation at Library and Archives Canada.)

———. "Post-Confederation Sources Relating to Indians and Inuit: Thematic Guide." (Unpublished finding aid available for consultation at Library and Archives Canada.)

Leslie, John and Ron Maguire. T*he Historical Development of the Indian Act*, 2nd edition. Ottawa, Ont.: Department of Indian Affairs and Northern Development, 1978.

Library and Archives Canada. *Guidelines for the Disclosure of Personal Information for Historical Research at the Public Archives of Canada*. Ottawa, Ont.: Library and Archives Canada, 1985.

Lovering, Cynthia, compiler. *General Guide Series — Government Archives Division*. Ottawa, Ont.: Library and Archives Canada, 1991.

Manitoba. Northern Affairs. *1998 Community Profiles: A Guide to the 56 Communities in Northern Manitoba Under the Jurisdiction of the Northern Affairs Act*. Winnipeg, Man.: Manitoba Northern Affairs, 1998. The now 62 communities are also available at <www.communityprofiles.mb.ca/first_nations.html>.

Mattison, David. *Catalogues, Guides and Inventories to the Archives of Alberta, British Columbia, Northwest Territories and the Yukon Territory: A Select Bibliography*. Occasional paper, 91-01. Vancouver, B.C.: Archives Association of British Columbia, 1991.

McCardle, Bennett. "Archival Records Relating to Native People in the Public Archives of Canada, the National Library of Canada, and the National Museum of Man: a Thematic Guide" (Unpublished finding aid available for consultation at the Claims and Historical Research Centre, Department of Indian and Northern Affairs, Ottawa.)

———. *Indian History and Claims: A Research Handbook*. 2 vols. Ottawa, Ont.: Research Branch, Department of Indian Affairs and Northern Development, 1982.

Merriman, Brenda Dougall. *Genealogy in Ontario: Searching the Records*, 3rd revised edition. Toronto, Ont.: Ontario Genealogical Society, 2002.

Morrison, James. *Aboriginal People in the Archives: A Guide to Sources in the Archives of Ontario*. Toronto: Archives of Ontario, 1992. Available at <www.archives.gov.on.ca/english/aborige/index.html>

Newfoundland and Labrador. Provincial Archives. *Aboriginal Thematic Guide.* St.John's, Nfld.: Provincial Archives of Newfoundland & Labrador, 1988.

Nin.Da.Waab.Jig. *Minishenhying Anishnaabe-aki or Walpole Island: the Soul of Indian Territory.* Wallaceburg, Ont.: Commercial Associates/Ross Roy Ltd., 1987.

Oliver, Edmund Henry. *The Canadian Northwest: Its Early Development and Legislative Records, Minutes of the Councils of the Red River Colony and the Northern Department of Rupert's Land.* 2 vols. Ottawa, Ont.: Public Archives of Canada, 1914-1915.

Ontario. Native Affairs Secretariat. *Akwesasne to Wunnumin Lake: Profiles of Aboriginal Communities in Ontario.* Toronto, Ont.: Ontario Native Affairs Secretariat and Ministry of Citizenship. 1992.

Owens, Brian M. and Claude M. Roberto, compilers. *A Guide to the Archives of the Oblates of Mary Immaculate, Province of Alberta-Saskatchewan.* Edmonton: Missionary Oblates, Grandin Province, 1989.

Prevost, Tony Jollay. *Indians from New York in Ontario and Quebec, Canada: A Genealogy Reference.* Volume 2. Bowie, Md.: Heritage Books, 1995.

Public Archives of Canada. *Guide to Canadian Ministries since Confederation, July 1, 1867–April 1, 1973.* Ottawa, Ont.: Public Archives Canada/Information Canada, 1974.

Ray, Arthur J. *Indians in the Fur Trade: Their Role As Trappers, Hunters and Middlemen in the Lands Southwest of Hudson Bay, 1660–1870.* Toronto, Ont.: University of Toronto Press, 1974.

Roy, Pierre Georges. *Les archives de la province et nos inventaires.* Québec, Qué.: s.n., 1926.

Tanner, Helen Hornbeck. *The Ojibwas: A Critical Bibliography.* Bloomington, Ind.: Indiana University Press, 1976.

Tanner, Helen Hornbeck (editor) and Miklos Pinther (cartographer). *Atlas of Great Lakes Indian History.* Chicago, Ill.; Norman, OK: published for the Newberry Library by the University of Oklahoma Press, 1987.

Titley, E. Brian. *A Narrow Vision: Duncan Campbell Scott and the Administration of Indian Affairs in Canada.* Vancouver: University of British Columbia Press, 1986.

Upton, Leslie F. S. *Micmacs and Colonists: Indian-White Relations in the Maritimes, 1713–1867.* Vancouver, B.C.: University of British Columbia Press, 1979.

White, James, editor. *Handbook of Indians in Canada.* [Published as an Appendix to the *10th Annual Report* of the Department of Marine and Fisheries/Canadian Parliament Session Papers No.21A]. Ottawa, Ont.: Geographic Board of Canada/C.H. Parmelee, 1913. Reprint edition: Toronto, Ont.: Coles Reprints, 1974.

Yukon. Archives. *Genealogical Sources Available at the Yukon Archives.* Rev. edn. Whitehorse, Yukon: Yukon Archives, 1998

———. *Yukon Native History and Culture: A Bibliography of Sources Available at the Yukon Archives.* Whitehorse, Yukon: Yukon Archives, 1987

Articles and Chapters

Faux, David K. "Documenting Six Nations Ancestry." *Families,* Vol.20, no.1 (1981)

Hall, David. "Clifford Sifton and Canadian Indian Administration, 1896-1905." *Prairie Forum*, Vol.2, nos 1-2 (1977)

Larmour, Jean. [two studies on] Edgar Dewdney in *Saskatchewan History*, No.23 (1970) and No.33 (1980)

Leighton, Douglas. "A Victorian Civil Servant at Work: Laurence Vankoughnet and the Canadian Indian Department, 1874-1893" in *As Long As the Sun Shines and the Water Flows*, edited by I.A.L. Getty and A.S. Lussier (Vancouver: University of British Columbia Press, 1983)

Looy, A.J. "Saskatchewan's First Indian Agent, M.G. Dickieson." *Saskatchewan History*, No.32 (1979)

Russell, Bill. "The White Man's Paper Burden: Aspects of Records Keeping in the Department of Indian Affairs, 1860-1914." *Archivaria*, No.19 (Winter 1984/1985)

Wilson, J.D. "'No blanket to be worn in school': the education of Indians in nineteenth-century Ontario" in *Indian Education in Canada*, Vol. 1: *The Legacy*, edited by J. Barman, Y. Hebert and D. McCaskill. (Vancouver: University of British Columbia, 1979)

On-line Resources

Library and Archives Canada's own Canadian Genealogy Centre Web site is <www.genealogy.gc.ca> where you can find the Aboriginal Peoples section and the specific guide "Researching Your Aboriginal Ancestry at Library and Archives Canada." A considerable amount of the content of that guide relates to RG 10 records.

The Annual Reports of the Department of Indian Affairs can be found at <www.collectionscanada.ca/indianaffairs>. The Annual Reports contain a surprising number of references to individual members of First Nations and are, of course, full of references to Department employees.

Aboriginal Peoples in the Archives: A Guide to Sources in the Archives of Ontario can be found on the Archives' Web site <www.archives.gov.on.ca/english/aborige/index.html>. Be aware that this guide was last updated in 1992 and some of the information may be out of date.

For a directory of archives in Canada go to <www.cdncouncilarchives.ca/directory.html>. There is also a listing at <www.archivescanada.ca/index2.html> the Canadian Archival Information Network (CAIN).

Index

More fine books from
The Ontario Genealogical Society
www.ogs.on.ca

Understanding Ontario First Nations Genealogy Records: Sources and Case Studies
Dr. David K. Faux
"His ... work is ... praiseworthy, a recommended acquisition for genealogical libraries." – *The New York Genealogical and Biographical Record*, March 2003. After the Revolutionary war in the United States, the people of the Six Nations, who had remained loyal to Britain, made their way to Ontario and eventually to the area in today's Brant County. In documenting his own family history, Dr. Faux discovered many unusual sources of genealogical data. In this useful work he shares his finds and suggests ways to go about your own search.
2002 136p 0-7779-2121-9 **$25.00**

Index to the Upper Canada Land Books
Susan Smart ed.
These indexes record all petitioners who came before the Executive Council of the Land Board of Upper Canada, as well as surnames found within the petition itself, and includes details such as petitioner's residence, occupation or location of the land grant. It also notes the petition number, which will lead the researcher to another set of records available on microfilm from the National Archives. The ten volumes covering 1787 to 1841 will be published over several years.

Volume 2, January 1798 to December 1805 over 11,000 names. 2004 0-7779-2140-5 **$38.00**
Volume 3, January 1806 to December 1816 over 11,000 names. 2001 313p 0-7779-2116-2 **$38.00**
Volume 4, January 1817 to December 1820 over 9,700 names. 2001 267p 0-7779-2118-9 **$38.00**
Volume 5, January 1821 to December 1826 over 9,800 names. 2002 360p 0-7779-2117-0 **$38.00**
Volume 6, January 1827 to December 1832 over 10,900 names. 2002 347p 0-7779-2126-X **$38.00**
Volume 7, January 1833 to December 1835 over 10,900 names. 2003 340p 0-7779-2132-4 **$38.00**
Volume 8, January 1836 to December 1838 over 9,600 names. 2003 323p 0-7779-2137-5 **$38.00**
Volume 9, January 1839 to February 1841 over 5,500 names. 2004 192p 0-7779-2139-1 **$25.00**

> *Volume 1 is coming Spring 2005*

An Index of Land Claim Certificates of Upper Canada Militiamen Who Served in the War of 1812–1814
Wilfred R. Lauber
During the War of 1812 citizen-soldiers served alongside British regular troops. Many who served were entitled to land grants and the records of those 4,500 grants, held in Library and Archives Canada, are here indexed. The author has made those records more accessible by giving exact archival references for obtaining copies of files and providing the militia unit in which a man served.
1995 136p 0-7779-0190-0 **$15.00**

Men of Upper Canada: Militia Nominal Rolls 1828–1829
Bruce S. Elliott, Dan Walker, Fawne Stratford-Devai
These lists identify and locate some 27,000 male inhabitants of Upper Canada, including officers and some reservists aged 40 to 60. The rolls constitute the closest thing to a province-wide census that survives for a genealogically difficult period, coming midway between the Loyalist influx of the 1780s and the first fully nominal census in 1852.
1995 376p 0-7779-0188-9 **$20.00**

About Genealogical Standards of Evidence: A Guide for Genealogists –rev'd 2nd ed.
Brenda Merriman
Genealogical evidence is the information or data that help us to *identify* an individual, or the relationship between individuals. In describing how we establish or argue point of identification through the use of various sources, we often see or hear — and use — such words as "evidence" or "proof" or "documentation." Because the genealogical community is constantly revising and updating how to establish such evidence, the author has completely revised and updated this essential tool.
2004 0-7779-2135-9 **rev. 2nd ed. $16.00**

Genealogy in Ontario: Searching the Records
Brenda Merriman
"...if you have Ontario roots/relations, you *must* own a copy of this first class guidebook." –Terrence M. Punch, CG(C), *The Nova Scotian Genealogist*
Now in its revised third edition, this book is a comprehensive guide through the genealogical resources of Ontario, first known as Upper Canada, then as Canada West. Here you'll find primary sources, finding aids, microform availability and significant secondary sources such as relevant articles and books. There's even help with accessing the records from a distance.
2002 278p 0-7779-2127-8 **rev. 3rd ed. $32.00**

Tools of the Trade for Canadian Genealogy –rev'd 2nd ed.
Althea Douglas
As she met people climbing their family trees, the author became aware of gaps in people's research knowledge. This volume will fill in some of those gaps relating to Canadian archives and records and provide ways to approach family history research in Canada, for both those who live here and those whose families moved through the country on their way to elsewhere. *Tools* gets the researcher thinking about **what** records were created, **who** kept the records, **why** there were kept, **where** they should turn up or where they may be lurking, and **why** some information does or does not survive.
2004 144p 0-7779-2134-0 **$21.95**